APOSTOLIC MANUALS OF THE EARLY CHURCH

THE DIDACHE, DIDASCALIA APOSTOLORUM, AND APOSTOLIC TRADITION

Apostolic Manuals of the Early Church

The Didache, Didascalia Apostolorum, and Apostolic Tradition

Early Church Fathers

TAN Books
Gastonia, North Carolina

This edition of *The Apostolic Manuals of the Early Church* is an original compilation retypeset from publicly available sources and published in 2025 by TAN Books. *The Didache* is from the 1886 Christian Literature Publishing Company edition of *Ante-Nicene Fathers* edited by Alexander Roberts, James Donaldson, and A. Cleveland Coxe. *The Didascalia Apostolorum* is from the 1929 Oxford: Clarendon Press edition translated by R. Hugh Connolly. *The Apostolic Tradition* is from the 1934 Cambridge University Press edition translated by Burton Scott Easton.

Cover design by Caroline Green

Cover image: *Christ Giving the Keys to St. Peter* by Peter Paul Rubens. Public domain via Wikimedia Commons.

ISBN: 978-1-5051-3728-6
ePUB ISBN: 978-1-5051-3887-0

Published in the United States by
TAN Books
PO Box 269
Gastonia, NC 28053

www.TANBooks.com

Printed in the United States of America

Contents

The *Didache*

The Catholic Teaching of the Twelve Holy Apostles and Disciples of Our Savior

Anonymous (1st century)

Chapter I

The Two Ways; The First Commandment

There are two ways, one of life and one of death; but a great difference between the two ways. The way of life, then, is this: First, *thou shalt love God who made thee*; second, *thy neighbour as thyself*; (cf. Lev. 19:18; Matt. 22:37, 39; Mark 12: 30, 31) and *all things whatsoever thou wouldst should not occur to thee, thou also to another do not do* (cf. Tobit 4:15; Matt. 7:12; Luke 6:31).

And of these sayings the teaching is this: "Bless them that curse you", and "pray for your enemies, and fast for them that persecute you" (Matt. 5:44). For "what thank is there, if ye love them that love you? Do not also the Gentiles do the same?" (Matt. 5:46) But "do ye love them that hate you"; (Luke 6:27) and ye shall not have an enemy. "Abstain thou from fleshly and worldly lusts" (1 Peter 2:11). If one give thee a "blow upon thy right cheek, turn to him the other also"; and thou shalt be perfect (Matt. 5:39, 48; Luke 6:29). If one "impress thee for one mile, go with him two". If one "take away thy cloak, give him also thy coat" (Matt. 5:40, 41). If one "take from thee thine own, ask it not back", (Luke 6:30) for indeed thou art not able.

"Give to every one that asketh thee, and ask it not back"; (Luke 6:30) for the Father willeth that to all should be given of our own blessings. Happy is he that giveth according to the commandment; for he is guiltless. Woe to him that receiveth; for if one having need receiveth, he is guiltless; but he that receiveth not having need, shall pay the penalty, why he received and for what, and, coming into straits (confinement), he shall be examined concerning the things which he hath done, and "he shall not escape thence until he pay back the last farthing". But also now concerning this, it hath been said, "Let thine alms sweat in thy hands, until thou know to whom thou shouldst give".

Chapter II

The Second Commandment: Grave Sin Forbidden

And the second commandment of the Teaching; You shall not commit murder, you shall not commit adultery, you shall not commit pederasty, you shall not commit fornication, you shall not steal, you shall not practice magic, you shall not practice witchcraft, you shall not murder a child by abortion nor kill that which is begotten. You shall not covet the things of your neighbour, you shall not forswear yourself, you shall not bear false witness, you shall not speak evil, you shall bear no grudge. You shall not be double-minded nor double-tongued; for to be double-tongued is a snare of death. Your speech shall not be false, nor empty, but fulfilled by deed. You shall not be covetous, nor rapacious, nor a hypocrite, nor evil disposed, nor haughty. You shall not take evil counsel against your neighbour. You shall not hate any man; but some you shall reprove, and concerning some you shall pray, and some you shall love more than your own life.

Chapter III

Other Sins Forbidden

My child, flee from every evil thing, and from every likeness of it. Be not prone to anger, for anger leads the way to murder; neither jealous, nor quarrelsome, nor of hot temper; for out of all these murders are engendered. My child, be not a lustful one; for lust leads the way to fornication; neither a filthy talker, nor of lofty eye; for out of all these adulteries are engendered.

My child, be not an observer of omens, since it leads the way to idolatry; neither an enchanter, nor an astrologer, nor a purifier, nor be willing to look at these things; for out of all these idolatry is engendered. My child, be not a liar, since a lie leads the way to theft; neither money-loving, nor vainglorious, for out of all these thefts are engendered.

My child, be not a murmurer, since it leads the way to blasphemy; neither self-willed nor evil-minded, for out of all these blasphemies are engendered. But be meek, since the meek shall inherit the earth. Be long-suffering and pitiful and guileless and gentle and good and always trembling at the words which you have heard. You shall not exalt yourself, nor give over-confidence to your soul. Your soul shall not be joined with lofty ones, but with just and lowly ones shall it have its intercourse. The workings that befall you receive as good, knowing that apart from God nothing comes to pass.

Chapter IV

Various Precepts

My child, him that speaks to you the word of God remember night and day; and you shall honour him as the Lord; for in the place whence lordly rule is uttered, there is the Lord. And you shall seek out day by day the faces of the saints, in order that you may rest upon their words. You shall not long for division, but shall bring those who contend to peace. You shall judge righteously, you shall not respect persons in reproving for transgressions. You shall not be undecided whether it shall be or not.

Be not a stretcher forth of the hands to receive and a drawer of them back to give. If you have anything, through your hands you shall give ransom for your sins. You shall not hesitate to give, nor murmur when you give; for you shall know who is the good repayer of the hire. You shall not turn away from him that is in want, but you shall share all things with your brother, and shall not say that they are your own; for if you are partakers in that which is immortal, how much more in things which are mortal?

You shall not remove your hand from your son or from your daughter, but from their youth shall teach them the fear of God. You shall not enjoin anything in your bitterness upon your bondman or maidservant, who hope in the same God, lest ever they shall fear not God who is over both; for he comes not to call according to the outward appearance, but unto them whom the Spirit has prepared. And you bondmen shall be subject to your masters as to a type of God, in modesty and fear. You shall hate all hypocrisy and everything which is not pleasing to the Lord. Forsake in no way the commandments of the Lord; but you shall keep what you have received, neither adding thereto nor taking away therefrom. In the church you shall acknowledge your transgressions, and you shall not come near for your prayer with an evil conscience. This is the way of life.

Chapter V

The Way of Death

And the way of death is this: First of all it is evil and accursed: murders, adultery, lust, fornication, thefts, idolatries, magic arts, witchcrafts, rape, false witness, hypocrisy, double-heartedness, deceit, haughtiness, depravity, self-will, greediness, filthy talking, jealousy, over-confidence, loftiness, boastfulness; persecutors of the good, hating truth, loving a lie, not knowing a reward for righteousness, not cleaving to good nor to righteous judgement, watching not for that which is good, but for that which is evil; from whom meekness and endurance are far, loving vanities, pursuing revenge, not pitying a poor man, not labouring for the afflicted, not knowing Him Who made them, murderers of children, destroyers of the handiwork of God, turning away from him who is in want, afflicting him who is distressed, advocates of the rich, lawless judges of the poor, utter sinners. Be delivered, children, from all these.

Chapter VI

Against False Teachers, and Food Offered to Idols

See that no one causes you to err from this way of the Teaching, since apart from God it teaches you. For if you are able to bear the entire yoke of the Lord, you will be perfect; but if you are not able to do this, do what you are able. And concerning food, bear what you are able; but against that which is sacrificed to idols be exceedingly careful; for it is the service of dead gods.

Chapter VII

Concerning Baptism

And concerning baptism, baptise this way: Having first said all these things, baptise into the name of the Father, and of the Son, and of the Holy Spirit, in living water. But if you have no living water, baptise into other water; and if you cannot do so in cold water, do so in warm. But if you have neither, pour out water three times upon the head into the name of Father and Son and Holy Spirit. But before the baptism let the baptiser fast, and the baptised, and whoever else can; but you shall order the baptised to fast one or two days before.

Chapter VIII

Fasting and Prayer (The Lord's Prayer)

But let not your fasts be with the hypocrites; for they fast on the second and fifth day of the week; but fast on the fourth day and the Preparation (Friday). Neither pray as the hypocrites; but as the Lord commanded in His Gospel, thus pray:

Our Father who art in heaven, hallowed be Your name. Your kingdom come. Your will be done, as in heaven, so on earth. Give us today our daily (needful) bread, and forgive us our debt as we also forgive our debtors. And bring us not into temptation, but deliver us from the evil one (or, evil); for Yours is the power and the glory forever.

Thrice in the day thus pray.

Chapter IX

The Thanksgiving (Eucharist)

Now concerning the Thanksgiving (Eucharist), thus give thanks. First, concerning the cup:

We thank you, our Father, for the holy vine of David Your servant, which You made known to us through Jesus Your Servant; to You be the glory forever.

And concerning the broken bread:

We thank You, our Father, for the life and knowledge which You made known to us through Jesus Your Servant; to You be the glory forever. Even as this broken bread was scattered over the hills, and was gathered together and became one, so let Your Church be gathered together from the ends of the earth into Your kingdom; for Yours is the glory and the power through Jesus Christ forever.

But let no one eat or drink of your Thanksgiving, but they who have been baptised into the name of the Lord; for concerning this also the Lord has said, *"Give not that which is holy to the dogs"* (Matt. 7:6).

Chapter X

Prayer After Communion

But after you are filled, thus give thanks:

We thank You, holy Father, for Your holy name which You caused to tabernacle in our hearts, and for the knowledge and faith and immortality, which You made known to us through Jesus Your Servant; to You be the glory forever. You, Master almighty, created all things for Your name's sake; You gave food and drink to men for enjoyment, that they might give thanks to You; but to us You freely gave spiritual food and drink and life eternal through Your Servant. Before all things we thank You that You are mighty; to You be the glory forever. Remember, Lord, Your Church, to deliver it from all evil and to make it perfect in Your love, and gather it from the four winds, sanctified for Your kingdom which You have prepared for it; for Yours is the power and the glory forever. Let grace come, and let this world pass away. Hosanna to the God (Son) of David! If any one is holy, let him come; if any one is not so, let him repent. *Maranatha*. Amen.

But permit the prophets to make Thanksgiving as much as they desire.

Chapter XI

Concerning Teachers, Apostles, and Prophets

Whosoever, therefore, comes and teaches you all these things that have been said before, receive him. But if the teacher himself turn and teach another doctrine to the destruction of this, hear him not; but if he teach so as to increase righteousness and the knowledge of the Lord, receive him as the Lord. But concerning the apostles and prophets, according to the decree of the Gospel, thus do.

Let every apostle that comes to you be received as the Lord. But he shall not remain except one day; but if there be need, also the next; but if he remain three days, he is a false prophet. And when the apostle goes away, let him take nothing but bread until he lodges; but if he ask money, he is a false prophet. And every prophet that speaks in the Spirit you shall neither try nor judge; for every sin shall be forgiven, but this sin shall not be forgiven. But not every one that speaks in the Spirit is a prophet; but only if he hold the ways of the Lord.

Therefore from their ways shall the false prophet and the prophet be known. And every prophet who orders a meal in the Spirit eats not from it, except indeed he be a false prophet; and every prophet who teaches the truth, if he do not what he teaches, is a false prophet. And every prophet, proved true, working unto the mystery of the Church in the world, yet not teaching others to do what he himself does, shall not be judged among you, for with God he has his judgement; for so did also the ancient prophets. But whoever says in the Spirit, Give me money, or something else, you shall not listen to him; but if he says to you to give for others' sake who are in need, let no one judge him.

Chapter XII

Reception of Christians

But let every one that comes in the name of the Lord be received, and afterwards you shall prove and know him; for you shall have understanding right and left. If he who comes is a wayfarer, assist him as far as you are able; but he shall not remain with you, except for two or three days, if need be. But if he wills to abide with you, being an artisan, let him work and eat; but if he has no trade, according to your understanding see to it that, as a Christian, he shall not live with you idle. But if he wills not to do, he is a Christ-monger. Watch that you keep aloof from such.

Chapter XIII

Support of Prophets

But every true prophet that wills to abide among you is worthy of his support. So also a true teacher is himself worthy, as the workman, of his support. Every first-fruit, therefore, of the products of wine-press and threshing-floor, of oxen and of sheep, you shall take and give to the prophets, for they are your high priests. But if you have not a prophet, give it to the poor. If you make a batch of dough, take the first-fruit and give according to the commandment. So also when you open a jar of wine or of oil, take the first-fruit and give it to the prophets; and of money (silver) and clothing and every possession, take the first-fruit, as it may seem good to you, and give according to the commandment.

Chapter XIV

Christian Assembly on the Lord's Day

But every Lord's day gather yourselves together, and break bread, and give thanksgiving after having confessed your transgressions, that your sacrifice may be pure. But let no one that is at variance with his fellow come together with you, until they be reconciled, that your sacrifice may not be profaned. For this is that which was spoken by the Lord: *"In every place and time offer to me a pure sacrifice; for I am a great King, says the Lord, and my name is wonderful among the nations"* (Malachi 1:11).

Chapter XV

Bishops and Deacons; Christian Reproof

Therefore, appoint for yourselves bishops and deacons worthy of the Lord, men meek, and not lovers of money, and truthful and proven; for they also render to you the service of prophets and teachers. Despise them not therefore, for they are your honoured ones, together with the prophets and teachers. And reprove one another, not in anger, but in peace, as you have it in the Gospel; but to every one that acts amiss against another, let no one speak, nor let him hear anything from you until he repents. But your prayers and alms and all your deeds so do, as you have it in the Gospel of our Lord.

Chapter XVI

Watchfulness; The Coming of the Lord

Watch for your life's sake. Let not your lamps be quenched, nor your loins unloosed; but be ready, for you know not the hour in which our Lord comes. But often shall you come together, seeking the things which are befitting to your souls: for the whole time of your faith will not profit you, if you be not made perfect in the last time.

For in the last days false prophets and corrupters shall be multiplied, and the sheep shall be turned into wolves, and love shall be turned into hate; for when lawlessness increases, they shall hate and persecute and betray one another, and then shall appear the world-deceiver as the Son of God, and shall do signs and wonders, and the earth shall be delivered into his hands, and he shall do iniquitous things which have never yet come to pass since the beginning.

Then shall the creation of men come into the fire of trial, and many shall be made to stumble and shall perish; but they that endure in their faith shall be saved from under the curse itself. And then shall appear the signs of the truth; first, the sign of an outspreading in heaven; then the sign of the sound of the trumpet; and the third, the resurrection of the dead; yet not of all, but as it is said: "The Lord shall come and all His saints with Him". Then shall the world see the Lord coming upon the clouds of heaven.

Didascalia Apostolorum

Anonymous (3rd century, Syrian)

Chapter I

On the simple and natural Law.

God's planting and the holy vineyard of His Catholic Church, the elect, who rely on the simplicity of the fear of the Lord, who by their faith inherit His everlasting kingdom, who have received the power and fellowship of His Holy Spirit (cf. 2 Cor. 13:13), and by Him are armed and made firm in the fear of Him, who are become partakers *in the sprinkling of the* (1 Pt. 1:2) pure and precious *blood of* the Great God, *Jesus Christ* (1 Pt. 1:17), who have received boldness to call the Almighty God Father, as joint heirs and partakers with His Son and His beloved (cf. Rom 8:17; Eph. 3:6) hear the Didascalia of God, you that hope and wait for His promises, which hath been written after the command of our Saviour and is in accord with His glorious words.

Give heed, children of God, and do all things so that you be obedient to God; and be you pleasing in all things to the Lord our God. For if any man run after iniquity and be contrary to the will of God, the same shall be accounted unto God as heathen and ungodly. Flee therefore and depart from all avarice and evil dealing. And you shall not desire that which is any man's, for it is written in the Law: *Thou shalt not desire aught of that which is thy neighbour's: neither his field, nor his wife, nor his servant, nor his maidservant, nor his ox, nor his ass, nor any thing of his possessions* (Ex. 20:17; Dt. 5:21). For all these desires are from the Evil One. For he that desires the wife of his companion, or his servant, or his maidservant, is already an adulterer and a thief, and is condemned of uncleanness, as they that lie with males, by our Lord and Teacher Jesus Christ: to whom is glory and honour for ever and ever, Amen. As also in the Gospel He renews and confirms and fulfils the Ten Words of the Law, saying: *For it is written in the Law: Thou shalt not commit adultery: but I say unto you* this,— who in the Law spake through Moses, but now myself say unto you: *Whosoever shall look upon the wife of his neighbour to desire her, hath already committed adultery with her in his heart* (Mt. 5:27–28). And thus was he who desired condemned as an adulterer. He also that desires the ox or the ass of his neighbour, it is to steal and to lead it away that he is minded. And he again that desires the field of his companion, does he not seek to straiten him in his boundary, and contrive that he may sell it to him for nothing? For this cause therefore come slayings and deaths and condemnations from God upon these persons.

But for men who obey God there is one law, simple and true and mild — without question, for Christians — this, that *what thou hatest that it should be done to thee by another, thou do not to another* (cf. Tob. 4:15). Thou wouldst not that a man should look upon thy wife evilly to corrupt her: neither look thou upon the wife of thy companion with evil intent. Thou wouldst not that a man should take away thy garment: neither do thou take away that of another. Thou wouldst not be reviled and insulted, or beaten: neither do thou to another anyone of 5 these things. But if a man revile thee, do thou bless him; for it is written in the Book of Numbers: *He that blesseth is blessed, and he that curseth is cursed* (cf. Num. 24:9; Gen. 27:29). And in the Gospel also it is written again: *Bless them that curse you* (Lk. 6:28; Mt. 5:44). And to them that do you evil, do not you evil; and *do good to them that hate you* (Lk. 6:27), and be patient and endure, for the Scripture saith: *Thou shalt not say*: *I wilt render to mine enemy evil, even as he hath done to me: but be patient, and the Lord will be thy helper, and will bring a recompense upon him that doeth thee evil* (Prov. 20:22). And again He saith in the Gospel: *Love them that hate you, and pray for them that curse you, and ye shall have no enemy* (Mt. 5:44; Lk 6:27; Did. 1:3). Let us attend then, our beloved, and understand these commandments and keep them, that we may be sons of the light (cf. Jn. 12:36; Eph. 5:8; 1 Th. 5:5).

Chapter II

Teaching every man that he should please his wife alone; and that he should not adorn himself and become a cause of stumbling to women; and that he should not love idleness; and that he should occupy himself with the Scriptures of life, and avoid profane writings and the bonds of the Second Legislation; and that he should not bathe in a bath with women; and that he should not give himself to the vice of harlots.

Bear with one another (cf. Gal. 6:2), O servants and sons of God. Let not a man despise or contemn his wife, nor be lifted up against her; but let him be merciful, and let his hand be open to give. And let him please his wife alone, and cherish her with honour; and let him study to be loved by her alone, and by none other. Adorn not thyself that a strange woman may see and desire thee. And if indeed thou be constrained by her and sin with her, death in fire shall come upon thee of a surety from God, even that which abides for ever, which is in sore and bitter fire; and thou shalt know and understand when thou art grievously tormented. But if thou do not this uncleanness, but put her from thee and deny her: in this only hast thou sinned, that by thy adornment thou hast caused the woman to be taken with the desire of thee; for thou hast caused her, to whom it so happened by reason of thee, to commit adultery through her desire. But not so art thou under sin, because thou didst not desire her: but there shall be mercy upon thee from the Lord, because thou didst not deliver thyself to her nor consent to her when she sent unto thee, neither in thought didst thou turn thyself to that woman who was taken with the desire of thee: but she on a sudden encountered thee, and was stricken in her thought and sent unto thee; but thou as a godfearing man didst deny her and avoid her, and didst not sin with her; but she was stricken in her heart, because thou art young and fair and comely, and didst adorn thyself and cause her to desire thee: and thou art found to be guilty of the sin of her to whom it so happened by reason of thy adornment. But entreat of the Lord God that sin be not ascribed to thee on this account. And if thou wouldst please God and not men, and lookest and hopest for the life and rest everlasting, adorn not thy natural beauty which is given thee from God, but with humility of neglect make it mean before men. In like manner also thou shalt not nourish the hair of thy head, but do thou shear it off; and thou shalt not comb and adorn it, nor anoint it, lest thou bring upon thee such women as ensnare, or are ensnared, by lust. Neither shalt thou put on fine raiment, nor be shod on thy feet with shoes which are fashioned according to the lust of folly; nor shalt thou put upon thy fingers rings of gold device: for all these things are the wiles of harlotry, and every thing that thou dost apart from nature. For to thee, a faithful man of God, it is not permitted to nourish the hair of thy head and to comb and smooth it, which is a wantonness of lust; neither shalt thou arrange and adorn it, nor adjust it so that it may be beautiful. And thou shalt not destroy the hairs of thy beard (cf. Lev. 19:27), nor alter the natural form of thy face and change it to other than God created it, because that thou desirest to please men. But if thou do these things, thy soul shall be deprived of life, and thou shalt be rejected before the Lord God. As a man therefore who would please God, take heed thou do no such things; and avoid all those things which the Lord hateth.

And thou shalt not stray and go about idly in the streets and see the vain spectacle of those who behave themselves evilly; but be thou always attending to thy craft and thy work, and be willing to do those things that are pleasing to God; and thou shalt be meditating constantly upon the words of the Lord. But if thou art rich and hast no need of a craft whereby to live, thou shalt not stray and go about vacantly; but be ever constant in drawing near to the faithful and to them that are like-minded with thee, and be meditating and learning with them the living words. And if not, sit at home and read the Law, and the Book of Kings and the Prophets, and the Gospel the fulfilment of these. But avoid all books of the heathen. For what hast thou to do with strange sayings or laws or lying prophecies, which also turn away from the faith them that are young? For what is wanting to thee in the word of God, that thou shouldst cast thyself upon these fables of the heathen? If thou wouldst read historical narratives, thou hast the Book of Kings; but if wise men and philosophers, thou hast the Prophets, wherein thou shalt find wisdom and understanding more than that of the wise men and philosophers; for they are the words of the one God, the only wise. And if thou wish for songs, thou hast the Psalms of David; but if thou wouldst read of the beginning of the world, thou hast the Genesis of the great Moses; and if laws and commandments, thou hast the glorious Law of the Lord God. All strange writings therefore, which are contrary to these, wholly avoid.

Yet when thou readest the Law, beware of the Second Legislation, that thou do but read it merely; but the commands and warnings that are therein much avoid, lest thou lead thyself astray and bind thyself with the bonds which may not be loosed of heavy burdens. For this cause therefore, if thou read the Second Legislation, consider this alone, that thou know and glorify God who delivered us from all these bonds. And have this set before thine eyes, that thou discern and know what (in the Law) is the Law, and what are the bonds that are in the Second Legislation, which after the Law were given to those who, in the Law and in the Second Legislation, committed so many sins in the wilderness. For the first Law is that which the Lord God spoke before the people had made the calf and served idols, which consists of the Ten Words and the Judgements. But after they had served idols, He justly laid upon them the bonds, as they were worthy. But do not thou therefore lay them upon thee; for our Saviour came for no other cause but to fulfil the Law, and to set us loose from the bonds of the Second Legislation. For He set loose from those bonds and thus called those who believe in Him, and said: *Come unto me, all ye that toil and are laden with heavy burdens, and I will give you rest* (Mt. 11:28). Do thou therefore, without the weight of these burdens, read the simple Law, which is in accord with the Gospel; and moreover the Gospel itself, and the Prophets; and the Book of Kings likewise, that thou mayest know that as many kings as were righteous were both advanced by the Lord God in this world, and continued in God's promise of everlasting life; but those kings who turned aside from God and served idols did justly, by a summary judgement, perish miserably, and were deprived of the kingdom of God, and instead of obtaining rest are punished. When therefore thou readest these things, thou wilt grow the more in faith and be improved.

And afterwards rise up, go forth to the market-place and bathe in a bath of men: but not in one of women, lest, when thou hast stripped thyself and shewn the nakedness of thy bare body, either thou be ensnared, or thou constrain another and she slip and be ensnared by thee. Beware of these things therefore, and thou shalt live unto God.

Learn, then, what saith the holy word in Wisdom: [1]*My Son, keep my words, and my commandments hide within thee. My son, honour the Lord, and be strengthened; and beside him thou shalt fear none other.* [2]*Keep my commandments, and live well, and my laws as the apple of thine eye;* [3]*and bind them upon thy fingers. and write them on the tables of thy heart.* [4]*And say to wisdom: Thou art my sister, and make known to thy soul understanding:* [5]*that she may keep thee from a strange and adulterous woman, whose words are flattering.* [6]*For from the window of her house and from the porch she looked forth into the streets;* [7] *and whomsoever she saw of the youths that are simple and lack understanding,* [8] *that pass in the street beside the corners of the paths of her house,* [9]*and speak in the darkness, at even and in the gloom of the stillness of the night:* [10] *then the woman went forth and met him, in the harlot's dress that fluttereth the heart of youths.* [11]*And she is wanton and bold and dissolute: and her feet cannot be quiet in her house;* [12]*but now she roameth abroad, and now she lurketh in the streets and in the corners.* [13]*And she caught him and kissed him, and made her face impudent, and said to him:* [14]*Sacrifices I have, even peace offerings, today do I pay my vows:* [15]*therefore am I come forth to meet thee; for I was looking to see thee, and I have found thee.* [16]*I have spread my couch with a coverlet, and with rugs of Egypt have I overlaid it:* 17*I have sprinkled saffron upon my couch, and cinnamon in my house.* 18 *Come, let us take our pleasure with love until morning, and let us embrace each other with desire,* 19*For my husband is not at home: he is gone a long journey,* 20*and hath taken a bag of money in his hand; and after many days will he come to his house.* 21*And she beguiled him with her many words, and with the flattery of her lips she drew him unto her.* 22*And he went after her like a simpleton, and as an ox that goeth to the slaughter, and as a dog to the leash,* 23*and as a hart stricken with an arrow; and he maketh haste as a bird to the snare: and he knew not that he went to the death of his soul.* 24*Now therefore, hear me, my son, and hearken to the words of my mouth.* 25*Let not thy heart incline to her ways, and draw not nigh to the door of her house, and go not astray in her path;* 26*for many slain hath she cast down, and there is no number to them that are slain by her.* 27*The ways of her house are the ways of Sheol, which bring down to the chambers of death* (Prov. 7:1–27). 1*My son, hearken to my wisdom, and to mine understanding bend thy mind:* 2*that my counsel may keep thee, and the knowledge of my lips which I command thee.* 3*For the lips of an adulterous woman drop honey, and with her flatteries she maketh sweet thy palate:* 4*but the latter end of them is more bitter than wormwood, and sharper than* *a two-edged sword.* [5]*For the feet of a foolish woman lead down to the chambers of Sheol them that cleave unto her: for there is no standing for her footsteps, nor treading in the land of life:* [6]*for her paths are error, and they are not known.* [7]*Now therefore, my son, hear me, and turn not aside from the words of my mouth.* [8]*Keep thy way far from her, and draw not nigh to the door of her house;* [9]*lest thou give thy life to others, and thy years to them that have no mercy;* [10]*and lest strangers be satisfied of thy strength, and thy revenues go into the houses of others:* [11]*and in thine old age thy soul repent thee, when the flesh of thy body is consumed,* [12]*and thou say: Why then did I hate correction, and my heart reject reproof;* [13]*and hearkened I not to the voice of my teachers, and to them that admonished me inclined not mine ears* [14]*I am come well-nigh into every evil* (Prov. 5:1–14).

And that we prolong not and extend the admonition of our teaching with many words, if we have left anything, do you as wise men choose for yourselves those things that are good from the holy Scriptures and from the Gospel of God, that you may be made firm, and may put away and cast from you all evil, and be found blameless in life everlasting with God.

Chapter III

An instruction to women, that they should please and honour their husbands alone, caring diligently and wisely for the work of their houses with attention; and that they should not bathe with men; and that they should not adorn themselves and become a cause of stumbling to men and ensnare them; and that they should be chaste and quiet, and not quarrel with their husbands.

And let a woman also be subject to her husband; *because the head of the woman is the man, and the head of a man* (Eph. 5:23; 1 Cor. 11:3) that walks in the way of justice *is Christ.* After the Lord Almighty, our God and the Father of the worlds, of the present and of that which is to come, and the Lord of every breath and of all powers, and His living and Holy Spirit — to whom is glory and honour for evermore, Amen — woman, fear thy husband and reverence him, and please him alone, and be ready to minister to him; and let thy hands be put forth to the wool, and thy mind be upon the spindle, as He saith in Wisdom: [10]*A valiant*

woman who shall find? For she is more worth than goodly
stones of great price; [11]*and the heart of her husband relieth*
upon her, and provision is not wanting to her, [12] *For she*
is a helper to her husband in all things, and causeth that
nothing be wanting to him in his living. [13]*She made wool*
and linen with her ready hands. [14]*She is become a good*
provider, as a merchant ship, and hath gathered all her
riches from afar. [15]*She rose up in the night and gave vict-*
uals to her household, and work to her handmaids. [16]*She*
looked upon a field, and bought it; and of the fruits of
her hands she planted a possession. [17]*She girded her loins*
with strength, and made firm her arms, [18]*and tasted that*
it is good to work: and her lamp was not put out all the
night long. [19]*Her arms she stretched forth with diligence,*
and her hands to the spindle. [20]*Her hands she extended to*
the poor, and of her fruits she gave to the needy. [21]*And her*
husband hath no anxiety for the house; for all his house-
hold have been clothed with a double raiment. [22]*She made*
for her husband garments of fine linen and scarlet: [23]*her*
husband is notable in the gates, when he sitteth in the
seat of the elders. [24]*She made in her house linen cloths*
and girdles, and sold to the Canaanites. [25]*Strength and*
comeliness are her raiment: and she shall rejoice in the last
day. [26]*She opened her mouth with wisdom and with pru-*
dence, and her tongue speaketh orderly. [27]*The ways of her*

house are strict: and bread she hath not eaten slothfully. She opened her mouth in wisdom, rightly: [28]*and the law of mercy is upon her tongue. Her sons rose up and were enriched, and praised he: and she shall rejoice in them in her last days. Her husband also congratulated her:* [29]*and her many daughters have gotten riches. And many great things she did, and she was exalted above all the women:* [30]*for a woman that feareth God shall be blessed, and the fear of the Lord shall glorify her.* [31]*Give unto her of her fruits, which are worthy of her lips, and let her be praised in the gates: and in every place let her husband be praised* (Prov. 31:10–31). And again: *A valiant woman is the crown of her husband* (Prov. 12:4).

You have heard, then, how great praise a chaste woman and one that loves her husband receives of the Lord God, one that is found faithful and is minded to please God. Thou therefore, O woman, shalt not adorn thyself that thou mayest please other men; and thou shalt not be plaited with the tresses of harlotry, nor put on the dress of harlotry, nor be shod with shoes so that thou resemble them that are such; lest thou bring upon thee those who are ensnared by these things. And if thou sin not thyself in this work of uncleanness, yet in this thou wilt have sinned, that thou hast constrained and caused that man to desire thee. But if thou also sin, thou hast destroyed thy life from God, and art become guilty also of the soul of that man. And moreover, when thou hast sinned with one, thou wilt grow reckless and go also to others; as in Wisdom He said: *When the wicked is come to the depth of evil, he contemneth and groweth reckless: and there cometh upon him dishonour and reproach* (Prov. 18:3). For one who is such that she is wholly stricken in her soul and taken with desire, leads captive the souls of them that lack understanding. But let us learn concerning these also, how the holy word in Wisdom exposes them; for it saith thus: *As a ring of gold in a swine's snout, so is beauty to a woman that doeth evil* (Prov. 11:22). And again: *As a worm in wood, so doth an evil woman destroy a man* (Prov 12.4). And again: [13]*A woman void of understanding and boastful cometh to want bread, and knoweth no shame.* [14]*For she sitteth in the street, by the door of her house, upon a high chair,* [15]*and calleth to them that pass by the way, and to them that walk in her paths, and saith:* [16]*Whoso among you is a simpleton, let him draw nigh to me; and to him that wanteth understanding I will say:* [17]*Touch lovingly the hidden bread, and stolen waters that are sweet.* [18]*And he knoweth not that valiant men perish with her, and come even to the depth of Sheol. But flee thou, and tarry not in that place; and lift not up thine eyes to look upon her* (Prov. 9:13–18). And again: *It is better to sit upon a corner of the roof than to dwell with a prating and quarrelsome woman within the house* (Prov. 21:9,19).

Thou therefore that art a Christian, do not imitate such women; but if thou wouldst be a faithful woman, please thy husband only. And when thou walkest in the street, cover thy head with thy robe, that by reason of thy veil thy great beauty may be hidden. And adorn not thy natural face; but walk with downcast looks, being veiled.

And take heed that thou bathe not in a bath with men. For when there is a women's bath in the city or in the village, a believing woman may not bathe in a bath with men. For if thou coverest thy face from strange men with a veil of modesty, how then canst thou go in with strange men to a bath? But if there is no women's bath, and thou art constrained to bathe in a bath of men and women, — which indeed is unfitting — bathe with modesty and shame, and with bashfulness and moderation: and not at all times, nor every day, and not at midday; but let there be an appointed season for thee to bathe at, to wit at the tenth hour. For it behoves thee, as a believing woman, by every means to fly from the vain and curious gaze of the many which is met with in a bath.

And thy strife with all, and especially with thy husband, check and restrain as a believing woman; lest thy husband, if he be a heathen, be offended by reason of thee and blaspheme against God, and thou receive a Woe from God: for, *Woe to them, by reason of whom the name of God is blasphemed among the gentiles* (Isa. 52:5; Rom. 2:24)*;* or lest again, if thy husband be a believer, he be constrained, as one who knows the Scriptures, and say to thee the word from Wisdom: *It is better to sit upon a corner of the roof than to dwell with a prating and quarrelsome woman within the house* (Prov. 21:9–10). For it behoves women by a veil of modesty and humility to shew fear of God, for the conversion and the increase of faith of them that are without, of men and women.

Now if we have admonished and instructed you in brief, our sisters and our daughters and our members, do you as wise women seek and choose out for yourselves those things that are good and honourable and without reproach in worldly conversation; and learn and know those things whereby you may arrive at the kingdom of our Lord, and may find rest, pleasing Him with good works.

Chapter IV

Teaching what manner of man he is that is chosen for the Bishopric, and of what sort his conduct should be.

But concerning the bishopric, hear ye. The pastor who is appointed bishop and head among the presbytery in the Church in every congregation, *it is required of him that he be blameless, in nothing reproachable* (1 Tim. 3:2; Tit. 1:7), one remote from all evil, a man not less than fifty years of age, who is now removed from the manners of youth (2 Tim. 2:22) and from the lusts of the Enemy, and from the slander and blasphemy of false brethren, which they bring against many because they understand not that word which is said in the Gospel: *Every one that shall say an idle word, shall give an answer concerning it to the Lord in the day of judgement: for from thy words thou shalt be justified, and from thy words thou shalt be condemned* (Mt. 12:36–37). But if it be possible, let him be instructed and apt to teach; but if he know not letters, let him be versed and skilled in the word, and let him be advanced in years.

But if the congregation be a small one, and there be not found a man advanced in years of whom they give testimony that he is wise and suitable to stand in the bishopric: but there be found there one who is young, of whom they that are with him give testimony that he is worthy to stand in the bishopric, and who, though he is young, yet by meekness and quietness of conduct shows maturity: let him be proved whether all give testimony concerning him, and so let him sit in peace. For Solomon also at the age of twelve years reigned over Israel; and Josiah at the age of eight years reigned with righteousness; and Joash likewise reigned when seven years old. Wherefore, even though he be young, yet let him be meek and fearful and quiet; for the Lord God said in Isaiah: *On whom shall I look and take pleasure in him, but on the quiet and meek, that trembleth at my words?* (Isa. 66:2; cf. Did. 3:8) And in the Gospel also He spoke thus: *Blessed are the meek, for they shall inherit the earth* (Mt. 5:5; cf. Did 3:7). And let him be merciful; for He said again in the Gospel thus: *Blessed are the merciful, for upon them there shall be mercy* (Mt. 5:7). And again let him be a peacemaker; for He saith: *Blessed are the peacemakers, for they shall be called the sons of God* (Mt. 5:9). And let him be clear of all evil and wrong and iniquity; for He saith again: *Blessed are the pure in heart, for they shall see God* (Mt. 5:8). And let him be *watchful and chaste and staid* and orderly; and let him not be turbulent, *and let him not be one that exceeds in wine*; *and let him not be a backbiter; but let him be quiet, and not be quarrelsome; and let him not be money-loving* (1 Tim. 3:2–3). *And let him not be youthful in mind, lest he be lifted up and fall into the judgement of Satan* (1 Tim. 3:6)*: for everyone that exalteth himself shall be humbled* (Lk. 14:11; 18:14). But it is required that the bishop be thus: *a man that hath taken one wife, that hath governed his house well* (1 Tim. 3:2, 4). And thus let him be proved when he receives the imposition of hands to sit in the office of the bishopric: whether he be chaste, and whether his wife also be a believer and chaste; and whether he has brought up his children in the fear of God, and admonished and taught them; and whether his household fear and reverence him, and all of them obey him. For if his household in the flesh withstand him and obey him not, how shall they that are without his house become his, and be subject to him (1 Tim. 3:4–5).

And let him be proved whether he be without blemish in the things of the world, and likewise in his body; for it is written: *See that there be no blemish in him that standeth up to be priest* (cf. Lev. 14:11). But let him be also without anger; for the Lord saith: *Anger destroyeth even the wise* (Prov. 15:1). And let him be merciful and gracious and full of love; for the Lord saith: *Love covereth a multitude of sins* (cf. 1 Pt. 4:8; Prov. 10:12). And let his hand be open to give; and let him love the orphans with the widows, and be a lover of the poor and of strangers. And let him be alert in his ministry, and constant in ministration; and let him be afflicting his soul, and not be one that is put to confusion. And let him know who is the more worthy to receive; for if there be a widow who has (some-what), or is able to nourish herself with that which she needs for her bodily sustenance; and there be another who, though she is not a widow, is in want, whether by reason of sickness, or of the rearing of children, or of bodily infirmity: to this latter rather let him stretch out his hand. But if there be any man who is dissolute, or drunken, or idle, and he be in straits for bodily nourishment, the same is not worthy of an alms, neither of the Church.

And let the bishop be also without respect of persons, and let him not defer to the rich nor favour them unduly; and let him not disregard or neglect the poor, nor be lifted up against them. And let him be scant and poor in his food and drink, that he may be able to be watchful in admonishing and correcting those who are undisciplined. And let him not be crafty and extravagant, nor luxurious, nor pleasure-loving, nor fond of dainty meats. And let him not be resentful, but let him be patient in his admonition; and let him be assiduous in his teaching, and constant in reading the divine Scriptures with diligence, that he may interpret and expound the Scriptures fittingly. And let him compare the Law and the Prophets with the Gospel, so that the sayings of the Law and the Prophets may be in accord with the Gospel. But before all let him be a good discriminator between the Law and the Second Legislation, that he may distinguish and show what is the Law of the faithful, and what are the bonds of them that believe not; lest anyone of those under thy authority take the bonds for the Law, and lay upon himself heavy burdens, and become a son of perdition. Be diligent therefore and attentive to the word, O bishop, so that, if thou canst, thou explain every saying: that with much doctrine thou mayest abundantly nourish and give drink to thy people; for it is written in Wisdom: *Be careful of the herb of the field, that thou mayest shear thy flock: and gather the grass of summer, that thou mayest have sheep for thy clothing: give attention and care to thy pasture, that thou mayest have lambs* (Prov. 27:25–26). Let not the bishop therefore be *a lover of filthy lucre* (1 Tim. 3:8), and especially from the heathen. Let him be suffering a wrong, and not doing a wrong; and let him not love riches. And let him not think ill of any man, nor bear false witness; and let him not be wrathful, nor quarrelsome; and let him not love the presidency; and let him not be double-minded nor double-tongued (cf. Did. 2:4), nor given to incline his ear to words of slander and murmuring; and let him be no respecter of persons. And let him not love the festivals of the heathen, nor occupy himself with vain error. And let him not be lustful, nor money-loving: for all these things are of the agency *or* demons.

Now all these things let the bishop command and enjoin upon all the people. And let him be wise and lowly; and let him be admonishing and teaching with the doctrine and discipline of God. And let him be of a noble mind, and aloof from all the evil artifices of this world, and from all the evil lust of the heathen. And let his mind be keen to discern, that he may know beforehand them that are evil: and do you keep yourselves from them. But let him be the friend of all, being a righteous judge. And whatever of good here be that is found in men, let the same be in the bishop. For when the pastor shall be remote from all evil, he will be able to constrain his disciples also and encourage them by his good manners to be imitators of his good works; as the Lord has said in the Twelve Prophets: *The people shall be even as the priest* (Hos. 4:9). For it behoves you to be an example to the people, for you also have Christ for an example. Be you therefore also a good example to your people, for the Lord said in Ezekiel: [1]*And the word of the Lord came unto me, saying:* [2]*Son of man, speak to the sons of thy people, and say unto them: When I bring the sword upon a land, let the people of that land take one man from among them and make him their watchman:* [3]*and he shall see the sword coming upon the land, and shall blow the trumpet and warn the people,* [4]*and everyone that heareth the sound of the trumpet shall give ear. And if he take not warning, and the sword come and take him away, his blood shall be upon his head.* [5]*Because he heard the sound of the trumpet, and took not warning, his blood shall be upon his head. But he that took warning hath delivered his soul.* [6]*But if the watchman see the sword coming, and blow not the trumpet, and the people be not warned, and the sword come and take away a soul from them: he hath been taken away in his sins, and his blood will I require at the hands of the watchman* (Ezk. 33:1–

6). Now the sword is the judgement, and the trumpet is the Gospel, but the watchman is the bishop who is set over the Church.

Chapter V

A teaching on judgement.

It behoves thee therefore, O bishop, when thou preachest, to testify and affirm concerning the judgement according as it is in the Gospel. For to thee also has the Lord said: *And thee, son of man, I have set as a watchman to the house of Israel; that thou mayest hear a word from my mouth, and give warning and preach it as from me. And when I say to the ungodly: The ungodly shall surely die, and thou preach not and say that the ungodly should depart from his iniquity: the ungodly shall die in his iniquity, and at thy hands will I require his blood. But if thou warn the ungodly from his way, and he take not warning: the ungodly shall die in his iniquity, and thou shalt deliver thy soul* (Ezk. 33:7–9). Wherefore you also, since to your account is laid the blame of them that sin in ignorance, do you preach and testify; and those who behave themselves without discipline admonish and rebuke openly. Now whereas we speak and repeat these things often, we are not blameworthy;

for through much teaching and hearing it happens that a man is put to shame, and does good and avoids evil. For the Lord also said in the Law: *Hear, O Israel* (Dt. 6:4); and unto this day they have not heard. And in the Gospel likewise He often proclaims and says; *Every one that hath ears to hear, let him hear* (Mt. 11:15; 13:9, etc.). But not even they have heard who thought that they heard; for they cast themselves swiftly into the dire destruction of heresy: upon whom the word of sentence is about to go forth. For we believe not, brethren, that when a man has (once) gone down into the water he will do again the abominable and filthy works of the ungodly heathen. For this is manifest and known to all, that whosoever does evil after baptism, the same is already condemned to the Gehenna of fire.

And we think indeed that the heathen also will blaspheme on this account, that we do not mix with them nor hold communication with them (cf. 1 Pt. 4:4). But through the falsehood of the heathen our brethren have the rather attained to the truth; for in the Gospel He saith thus: *Blessed are ye when they shall revile you, and persecute you, and speak against you every evil word for my sake, falsely. But do ye rejoice and be glad, for your reward is great in heaven: for so did their fathers persecute the prophets* (Mt. 5:11–12; Lk. 6:23). If therefore they shall blaspheme against any man falsely, blessed is he (cf. 1 Pt. 3:14), even because that he is tempted; for the Scripture has said: *A man that is not tempted, neither is he approved* (cf. Jas. 1:12; Sir. 34:10). But if a man be convicted of doing the works of iniquity, he is no Christian but a liar, and he holds the fear of the Lord in hypocrisy. Wherefore these persons, when they have been exposed and convicted by the truth openly, let, the bishop who is without offence and without hypocrisy avoid.

But if the bishop himself is not of a clean conscience, and accepts persons for the sake of filthy lucre, or for the sake of the presents which he receives, and spares one who impiously sins, and suffers him to remain in the Church: such a bishop has polluted his congregation with God; yea, and with men also, and with many of the receivers who are young in their minds, or with the hearers; and youths and maidens beside he destroys with him. For by reason of the lewdness of an ungodly man, when they have seen such a one in their midst they too will doubt in their soul, and will imitate him, and themselves also will stumble and be taken with the same malady, and will perish with him. But if he who sins sees that the bishop and the deacons are clear of reproach, and the whole flock pure: first of all he will not dare to enter the congregation, because he is reproved by his conscience; but if it should happen that he is bold, and comes to the Church in his arrogance, and he is reproved and rebuked by the bishop, and looking upon all present finds no offence in any of them, neither in the bishop nor in those who are with him: he will then be put to confusion, and will go forth quietly, in great shame, weeping and in remorse of soul; and so shall the flock remain pure. Moreover, when he is gone out he will repent of his sin and weep and sigh before God, and there shall be hope for him. And the whole flock itself also, when it sees the weeping and tears of that man, will fear, knowing and understanding that everyone who sins perishes.

Wherefore, O bishop, strive to be pure in thy works. And know thy place, that thou art set in the likeness of God Almighty, and holdest the place of God Almighty; and so sit in the Church and teach as having authority to judge them that sin in the room of God Almighty. For to you bishops it is said in the Gospel: *That which ye shall bind on earth, shall be bound in heaven* (Mt. 18:18).

Chapter VI

Concerning transgressors, and concerning those who repent.

Judge therefore, O bishop, strictly as God Almighty; and those who repent receive with mercy as God Almighty. And rebuke and exhort and teach; for the Lord God also with an oath promised forgiveness to them that have sinned, as He said in Ezekiel: *And thou, son of man, say to the house of Israel: Ye have said thus: Our crimes and our sins are upon us, and in them we are wasted away: how then can we live? Say unto them: As I live, saith the Lord Adonai, I desire not the death of the sinner, but that the wicked return from his evil way and live. Return, therefore, and be converted from your evil ways, and ye shall not die, O house of Israel.* (Ezk. 33:10–11) Here, then, He gave hope to them that sin, when they shall have repented, that they may have salvation by their repentance, and may not despair of themselves and continue in their sins and further add to them, but may repent and sigh and weep for their sins, and be converted with all their heart. (cf. Hermas Mand. 12:6–2)

But let them that have not sinned continue without sin, lest they also come to have need of weeping and sighs and sorrow, and of forgiveness. For whence knowest thou, O man that sinnest, how many are the days of thy life in this world, that thou mayest repent? For thou knowest not thy exit from the world, whether haply thou die in thy sins and there be no more repentance for thee; as it is said in David: *In Sheol who shall confess to thee?* (Ps. 6:6) Wherefore he remains without danger, whosoever spares his soul and remains without sin: so that the righteousness also which was done by him in time past may be preserved to him.

Do thou therefore, O bishop, thus judge: first of all strictly; and afterwards receive the sinner with mercy and compassion, when he promises to repent. And rebuke and afflict him, and afterwards be entreated of him, because of the word which is spoken in David thus: *Deliver not up the soul that confesseth to thee.* (Ps. 73(74):19) And in Jeremiah again He speaks thus concerning the repentance of them that sin: *Shall he that is fallen not rise up? or he that is turned away not return?*

Wherefore are my people turned away with a shameless perversion, and are held fast in their own devices, and have refused to repent and to return? (Jer. 8:4–5) For this cause, then, receive him that repents without hesitating ever so little; and be not hindered by those who are without mercy, who say: ‘ It is not fitting that we should be defiled with these. For the Lord God has said: *The fathers shall not die for the sons, nor the sons for the fathers.* (Dt 24.16) And again in Ezekiel He speaketh thus: *And the word of the Lord came unto me saying: Son of man, if a land sin against me, and do iniquity before me, I will stretch forth my hand against her, and will destroy out of her the staff of bread, and will send a famine upon her, and will destroy out of her men and beasts. But if there be in her these three men, Noah and Daniel and Job, they by their righteousness shall deliver their souls, saith the Lord Adonai.* (Ezk. 14:12–14) The Scripture, then, has shown clearly that if there be found a righteous man with an ungodly, he shall not perish with him, but every man shall be saved by his righteousness: and if he is hindered, it is by his own sins that he is hindered. And again in Wisdom He saith: *Every man is tied with the cord of his sins.* (Prov. 5:22) Each one therefore of the laity is to render an account of his own sins; and a man is not hurt by reason of the sins of others. For neither did Judas harm us at all when he was praying with us, but he alone perished. And in the ark, Noah and his two sons who were saved alive, they were blessed; but Ham, his other son, was not blessed, but his seed was cursed; (Gen. 9:25) and the animals that went in, animals they came forth.

It behoves you not therefore to hearken to those who desire to put to death, and hate their brethren and love accusations, and are ready to slay on any pretext: for one shall not die for another. But do you help them that are sore sick and exposed to danger and are sinning, that you may deliver them from death; and do not according to the hardness of heart and the word and thought of men, but according to the will and command of the Lord our God. For it behoves thee not, O bishop, that being the head thou shouldst obey the tail, that is a layman, a contentious man who desires the destruction of another; but do thou regard only the word of the Lord God. And concerning this, that men are not to suppose that they perish or are defiled by the sins of others, He again cut off their evil thought, and by Ezekiel also the Lord our God spoke thus: [1]*And the word of the Lord came unto me, saying:* [2]*Son of man, why use ye this proverb in the land of Israel, and say: The*

fathers do eat sour grapes, and their sons' teeth are on edge?
[3]As I live, saith the Lord Adonai, there shall no more be any that useth this proverb in Israel. [4]For all the souls are mine: as the soul of the father is mine, so also the soul of the son is mine. The soul that sinneth, the same shall die. [5]And a man, if he be righteous, and do judgement and righteousness, [6]and eat not upon the mountains, and lift not up his eyes to the idols of the house of Israel, and defile not the wife of his neighbour, and come not near to a woman in her menstruation, [7]and treat no man with violence, and restore the pledge of his debtor which he hath taken, and clothe the naked with a garment, [8]and give not out his money on usury, and receive not back with overcharge, and turn away his hand from iniquity, and judge right judgement betwixt a man and his neighbour,
[9]and walk in my laws, and keep my judgements and do them: this man is righteous, he shall surely live, saith the Lord Adonai, [10]And if he beget an evil son, that sheddeth blood and doeth iniquity, [11]and walketh not in the way of his righteous father, and eateth upon the mountains, and defileth his neighbour's wife, [12]and evil entreateth the poor and needy, and committeth robbery, and restoreth not the pledge which he hath taken, and lifteth up his eyes to idols, and doeth iniquity, [13]and giveth out his money on usury, and receiveth back with overcharge: this man shall

not live: because he hath done all this iniquity, he shall
surely die, and his blood shall be upon him. [14]*But if he*
beget a son, and he see those sins which his father did,
and fear and do not the like of them, [15]*and eat not upon*
the mountains, and lift not up his eyes to the idols of the
house of Israel, and defile not his neighbour's wife, [16]*and*
evil entreat no man, and take not a pledge, and commit
not robbery, and give his bread to the hungry, and clothe
the naked with a garment, [17]*and turn away his hand from*
iniquity, and receive not usury and overcharge, and do
righteousness and walk in my laws: this man shall not die
for the iniquity of his father, but he shall surely live. [18]*But*
his father, because he indeed committed oppression and
robbery, and did not good to my people, shall die for his
iniquity. [19]*And ye say: Wherefore is not the son requited for*
the iniquity of his father? Because the son did righteousness
and mercy, and kept all my commandments and did them,
he shall surely live: [20]*the soul that sinneth, the same shall*
die. A son shall not be requited for the sins of his father;
and a father shall not be requited for the sins of his son.
The righteousness of the righteous shall be upon him; and
the iniquity of the ungodly shall be upon him. [21]*And if the*
ungodly shall turn away from all his iniquity which he
did, and keep all my commandments, and do judgement
and righteousness, he shall surely live and not die; [22]*and*

all the iniquity which he did shall not be remembered
unto him: for the righteousness which he did, for the same
he shall live. 23 *For I desire not the death of the sinner, saith*
the Lord Adonai: but everyone that shall turn from his evil
way shall live. 24 *And if the righteous turn away from his*
righteousness, and do iniquity according to all the iniquity
which the ungodly did: all his righteousness which he did
shall not be remembered unto him, but for the iniquity
which he did, and for the sins which he sinned, for the
same he shall die. 25 *And they have said: The way of the*
Lord is not well. Hear ye, house of Israel: my way is well,
but your own ways are not well. 26 *And if the righteous*
shall turn away from his righteousness and do iniquity:
for the iniquity which he hath done he shall die. 27 *And if*
the ungodly shall turn away from his iniquity which he
did, and shall do judgement and righteousness: this man
hath delivered his soul. 28 *Because he turned away from all*
the iniquity which he did, he shall surely live and not die.
29 *And the house of Israel say: The way of the Lord is not*
well. My way is well, O house of Israel, but your own ways
are not well. 30 *Therefore will I judge every man of you*
according to his ways, saith the Lord Adonai. Return and
be converted from all your iniquity and your wickedness,
lest these things be unto you for an evil torment. 31 *And*
cast away and put from you all the wickedness which ye

have done, and make to yourselves a new heart and a new spirit, and ye shall not die, O house of Israel: [32]*for I desire not the death of the sinner, saith the Lord Adonai*: *but do ye return and live.* (Ezk. 18:1–32)

You see, beloved and dear children, how abundant are the mercies of the Lord our God and His goodness and loving-kindness towards us, and how He exhorts them that have sinned to repent. And in many places He speaks of these things; and He gives no place to the thought of those who are hard of heart and wish to judge strictly and without mercy, and to cast away altogether them that have sinned as though there were no repentance for them. But God is not so, but even sinners He calls to repentance and gives them hope; and those who have not sinned He teaches, and tells them that they should not suppose that we bear or partake in the sins of others. Simply, then, receive them that repent, rejoicing. For He spoke again in the same prophet concerning repentance thus: [12]*And thou, son of man, say to the sons of thy people: The righteousness of the righteous shall not deliver him in the day that he doeth wickedly; and the iniquity of the ungodly shall not hurt him in the day that he returneth from his iniquity: and the righteous cannot live in the day that he sinneth.*

[13]*And when I shall say to the righteous that he shall surely live, and he rely upon his righteousness and do iniquity: all his righteousness shall not be remembered unto him, but for the iniquity which he hath done, for the same he shall die.* [14]*And when I shall say to the ungodly: Thou shalt surely die; and he turn from his sin and do judgement and righteousness,* [15]*and return the pledge which he hath taken, and restore that which he hath robbed, and walk in the judgements and commandments of life so that he do no iniquity: he shall surely live and not die,* [16]*and all his sins which he sinned shall not be remembered unto him: he hath done judgement and righteousness, he shall surely live.* [17]*And the sons of thy people say: The way of the Lord Adonai is not well. Say unto them: It is your own ways are not well:* [18]*for if the righteous shall turn away from his righteousness and do iniquity, he shall surely die for his iniquity;* [19]*and if the ungodly shall turn away from his iniquity and do judgement and righteousness, for the same he shall live.* (Ezk. 33:12–19)

It behoves you then, O bishops, to judge according to the Scriptures those who sin, with gentleness and with mercy. For if, when a man is walking by the brink of a river and is ready to slip, thou by suffering him to slip hast thrust and cast him into the river, thou hast also committed murder. But if a man were to slip on the brink of a river and be near to perish, thou wouldst quickly reach out a hand to him and draw him out, lest he perish altogether. So do therefore with the sinner; that both thy people may learn and understand, and he also that sins may not utterly perish.

But when thou hast seen one who has sinned, be stern with him, and command that they put him forth; and when he is gone forth let them be stern with him, and take him to task, and keep him without the Church; and then let them come in and plead for him. For our Saviour Himself also was pleading with His Father for sinners, as it is written in the Gospel: *My Father, they know not what they do, neither what they speak: but if it be possible, do Thou forgive them.* (cf. Lk. 23:34, Mt. 26:39, 1 Tim. 1:7) And then do thou, O bishop, command him to come in, and examine him whether he be repentant. And if he is worthy to be received into the Church, appoint him days of fasting according to his offence, two or three weeks, or five, or seven; and so dismiss him that he may depart, saying to him whatever is right for admonition and instruction; and rebuke him, and say to him that he be by himself in humiliation, and that he beg and beseech during the days of his fast that he may be found worthy of the forgiveness of sins: as it is written in Genesis: *Hast thou sinned? be silent: thy repentance shall be with thee, and thou shalt have power over it.* (Gen. 4:7) To Mary the sister of Moses also, when she had spoken against Moses, and afterwards repented and was held worthy of forgiveness, it was said of the Lord: *If her father had but spit in her face, it were right for her to be ashamed, and to be separate seven days without the camp, and then to come in.* (Num. 12:14) So it behoves you also to do: to put forth from the Church those who promise to repent of their sins for a space proportionate to their offences: and afterwards do you receive them as merciful fathers.

But if the bishop be in himself a cause of offence, how can he stand up and make inquisition of any man's misdeeds, or rebuke him and give sentence upon him? For by reason of partiality, or of the presents which they receive — either he or the deacons, whose conscience is not pure — they (the deacons) cannot exert themselves to help the bishop; for they are afraid lest they should hear from the sinner, as from an insolent man, that word which is written in the Gospel: *Why seest thou the mote that is in thy brother's eye, and perceivest not the beam that is in thine own eye? Thou hypo-*

crite, cast out first the beam from thine eye; and then shalt thou perceive to cast the mote out of thy brother's eye. (Mt. 8:3, 5; Lk. 6:41–42) The reason, then, that the bishop, with his deacons, is afraid, is lest they should hear from the sinner, as from an insolent man, that word of the Lord. For he knows not that it is a perilous thing for a man to speak against the bishop, and that he (the bishop) may be made an offence throughout the whole of that district. For one who has been sinning lacks understanding, and no more spares his soul. Hence, for whatever cause it be that the bishop is afraid, he feigns not to have knowledge of him who sins, and passes him over and rebukes and corrects him not. And hence Satan, when he has found him an occasion by means of one, gets power over others also — which God forbid that it should come about — and so it happens that the flock becomes such that it can no longer be set right. For when there are found many that sin, evil waxes strong; and whereas they that sin are not corrected and reproved that they should repent, this becomes to all an inducement to sin: and that which is said is fulfilled: *My house is called a house of prayer, but ye have made it a den of thieves.* (Mt. 21:13; Lk. 19:46) But if the bishop keeps not silent from them that sin, but rebukes and reproves and corrects and admonishes and afflicts him that sins, he casts dread and fear upon others also. For it behoves the bishop to be by his doctrine a restrainer of sins and an example and encourager of righteousness, and by the admonition of his teaching a director of good works, and one who lauds and magnifies the good things which are to come and are promised by God in the place of life everlasting: a proclaimer also of the wrath to come in the judgement of God, with threatening of the grievous fire which is unquenchable and intolerable. And let him know the meaning of God's will, that he despise no man; because our Saviour has said: *See that ye despise not any of these little ones that believe in me.* (Mt. 18:10; cf. v. 6)

Let the bishop therefore be careful of all, both of them that have not sinned, that they may continue as they are without sin, and of them that have sinned, that they may repent, and that he may grant them forgiveness of sins, as it is written in Isaiah that the Lord saith: *Loose every bond of iniquity, and sever all bands of violence and extortion.* (Isa. 58:6)

Chapter VII

To Bishops.

Do thou therefore, O bishop, teach and rebuke, and loose by forgiveness. And know thy place, that it is that of God Almighty, and that thou hast received authority to forgive sins. For to you bishops it was said: *All that ye shall bind on earth, it shall be bound in heaven; and all that ye shall loose, it shall be loosed.* (Mt. 18:18) As therefore thou hast authority to loose, know thyself and thy manners and thy conversation in this life, that they be worthy of thy place. But without sin there is none among men, (cf. 3 Kgms. 8:46; 2 Chr. 6:36) for it is written: *There is no man pure of defilement, not even though his life in the world be but one day.* (Job 14:4–5) Therefore the life and manner of conversation of the just men and patriarchs was written, that it might be known that in each one of them there was found at least some small sin; that it might be understood that the Lord God alone is without sin, as He said in David: *That thou mayest be justified in thy words, and prevail in thy judgements.* (Ps. 50(51):6) For the little defilement of the just is to us a solace and an encouragement, and a source of trust that we also, if we sin but a little, have a hope of obtaining forgiveness.

There is no man, then, without sin. But do thou strive according to thy power to be *in nothing reproachable.* (1 Tim. 3:2) And have a care of all, that none may stumble and perish by reason of thee. For a layman has the care of himself alone, but thou carriest the burden of all. And very great is the load that thou bearest; *for to whom the Lord hath given much, much also will he require at his hand.* (Lk. 12:48) As therefore thou carriest the burden of all, be watchful; for it is written: *The Lord said unto Moses: Thou and Aaron shall take upon you the sins of the priesthood.* (Num. 18:1) For as thou art to render an account for many, so be careful of all; for those that are sound thou shalt preserve, but those that have sinned do thou admonish and rebuke and afflict; and afterwards ease them with forgiveness. And when he that sinned has repented and wept, receive him; and while the whole people prays over him, lay hand upon him, and suffer him henceforth to be in the Church. But those who are drowsy and slack do thou bring back and stir up and make firm, and exhort

them and make them sound: for thou knowest what
reward thou hast if thou do thus; but if thou neglect it,
danger shall come upon thee; for the Lord spoke thus
in Ezekiel concerning those bishops who neglect their
people: 1 *And the word of the Lord came unto me, saying:*
2 *Son of man, prophesy against the shepherds of Israel, and*
say to them: Thus saith the Lord Adonai: Woe unto the
shepherds of Israel, who feed themselves; and my sheep the
shepherds have not fed. 3 *The milk ye eat, and with the*
wool ye are clothed, and that which is fat ye kill and the
sheep ye feed not. 4 *That which was sick ye healed not, and*
that which was weak ye strengthened not, and that which
was broken ye bound not up, and that which was gone
astray ye brought not back, and that which was lost ye
sought not out; but with force and with derision ye have
subdued them. 5 *And my sheep were scattered for lack of*
a shepherd, and became meat for every beast of the field.
6 *And my sheep were scattered and gone astray on an the*
high mountains and on an the high hills, and on an the
face of the land were my sheep scattered, and there was
none to require and seek. 7 *Wherefore, ye shepherds, hear*
the word of the Lord Adonai. 8 *Forasmuch as my sheep are*
become a spoil and meat to every beast of the field for lack
of a shepherd, and the shepherds have not sought my sheep,
but the shepherds have fed themselves, and my sheep the

shepherds have not fed: 9 therefore, ye shepherds, hear the
word of the Lord. 10 Thus saith the Lord Adonai: Behold, I
am against the shepherds, and I wilt seek my sheep at their
hands; and I will cause them to cease, that henceforth they
feed not my sheep: and the shepherds shalt no more feed
themselves; but I will deliver my sheep out of their hands,
and they shall no more be to them for meat. 11 For thus
saith the Lord Adonai: Therefore, behold, I wilt seek my
sheep and visit them: 12 as a shepherd visiteth his sheep in
the day of tempest, when he is in their midst, so will I visit
my sheep. And I will gather them together from all places
wherein they were scattered in the day of cloud and thick
darkness, 13 and I will bring them forth from the peoples,
and gather them from the lands, and bring them into their
land; and I will feed them in the mountains of Israel, and
in all the waste places of the land. 14 And in a good and fat
pasture will I feed them, and in the mountains of the Most
High of Israel shall be the glory of their beauty. There shall
they be encamped in a good encampment, and in a fat
pasture shall they be fed in the mountains of Israel. 15 I will
feed my sheep, and I will establish them, saith the Lord
Adonai: 16 that which is lost will I seek, and that which
is gone astray will I bring back, and that which is broken
will I bind up, and that which is sick will I strengthen,
and that which is fat and sound will I keep:? and I will

*feed them in judgement. [17]And ye, my sheep, the sheep of
my flock, thus saith the Lord Adonai: Behold, I will judge
between ewe and ewe, and between ram and ram. [18]Is this
a small thing to you, that ye devour a good and fat pasture,
and the residue of your pasture ye trample upon with your
feet, [19]and my sheep did drink that which was trodden
with your feet. [20]Wherefore thus saith the Lord Adonai:
Behold, I will judge between ewe and ewe, and between
them that are sick: [21]because that ye were thrusting them
with your sides and with your shoulders, and with your
horns ye were butting all the sick ones, until ye had scattered them abroad. [22]And I will deliver my sheep, and
they shall no more be for a spoil: and I will judge between
ewe and ewe. [23]And I will set over them one shepherd, and
he shall feed them, and he shall be their shepherd; [24]and
David my servant shall be their ruler in their midst: I the
Lord have spoken it. [25]And I will make for them a covenant of peace, and will cause evil beasts to cease from the
land; and they shall dwell in the wilderness securely, and
sleep in the woods. [26]And I will give to them round about
my mountain a blessing; and I will send down rain in
its season, and it shall be rain of blessing. [27]And the trees
of the field shall give their fruits, and the land shall give
its increase. And they shall dwell in their land securely:
and they shall know that I am the Lord, when I shall cut*

the thongs of their yoke. And I will deliver them from the hand of them that subdued them, [28]*and they shall no more be for a prey to the peoples, and the beasts of the field shall no more devour them; but they shall lie down securely, and there shall be none to make them afraid.* [29]*And I will establish for them a plantation for renown; and they shall no more be few and forsaken in the land, and they shall no more bear the shame of the peoples.* [30]*And they shall know that I am the Lord their God with them, and they are my people of the house of Israel, saith the Lord Adonai.* [31]*And ye my sheep, the sheep of my flock, are men, and I am your God, saith the Lord Adonai.* (Ezek. 34:1–31)

Hear, then, ye bishops, and hear, ye laymen, how the Lord saith: *I will judge between ram and ram, and between ewe and ewe*; (Ezk. 34:17) that is, between bishop and bishop, and between layman and layman: whether layman loves layman, and whether again the layman loves the bishop and honours and fears him as father and lord, and as God after God Almighty; for to the bishop it was said through the apostles: *Everyone that heareth you, heareth me; and everyone that rejecteth you rejecteth me, and him that sent me*: (Lk. 10:16) and again, whether the bishop loves the laity as his children, and cherishes and keeps them warm with loving care, as eggs from which young birds are to come; or broods over them and cherishes them as young birds, for the rearing up of winged fowl. Teach, then, and admonish all; and them that deserve rebuke, rebuke and afflict: but unto conversion and not unto destruction; and admonish unto repentance and correct them, so that thou make their ways straight and fair, and order well the conduct of their life in the world.

That which is whole preserve: (Ezk. 34:16) that is, him that is established in the faith guard watchfully; and shepherd the whole people in peace. *And that which is weak strengthen*: (Ezk. 34:4) that is, him that is tempted confirm with admonition. *And that which is sick heal*: (Ezk. 34:4) that is, him that is sick with doubting of his faith, heal with doctrine. *And that which is broken bind up*: (Ezk. 34:4, 16) that is, him that is stricken or buffeted or broken by his sins, and halts from the right way, bind up; that is, with the exhortation of admonition cure him, and lighten him of his transgressions, and comfort him and show him that there is hope for him; and bind him up and heal him and bring him into the Church. *And that which is gone astray bring back*: (Ezk. 34:4, 16) that is, him that was left in sins and was put forth for reproof, leave not without, but teach and admonish him, and bring him back and receive him into thy flock, that is, into the people of the Church. *And that which is lost seek out*: (Ezk. 34:4, 16) that is, him who by reason of the multitude of his transgressions has despaired and abandoned himself to destruction, suffer not to perish altogether, lest through utter neglect and indifference he fall asleep, and under the weight of his sleep forget his life, and hold aloof and depart from his flock, that is from the Church, and come to perdition. For when he shall be without the fold and removed from the flock, wolves will devour him while he is astray, and he will perish utterly. But do thou seek him out, and admonish and teach him, and bring him back; and visit him, and encourage him to be wakeful, and let him know that there is hope for him. And cut away this from men's thought, that they should say or imagine that which has already been rehearsed: *Our crimes and our sins are upon us, and in them we are wasted away: how then can we live?* (Ezk. 33:10) For they ought not to say or to imagine these things; and they are not to think that their hope is cut off by reason of the multitude of their sins; but they are to know that the mercies of God are many, for that with an oath and with gracious intent He has promised forgiveness to them that sin.

But if a man sin and know not the Scriptures, and is not aware of the patience and mercy of God, and knows not the limit of forgiveness and repentance: by this very thing, that he is ignorant, he perishes. Do thou therefore as a compassionate shepherd, full of love and mercy and careful of his flock, visit and count thy flock, and seek that which is gone astray; as said the Lord God, Jesus Christ our good Teacher and Saviour: 'Leave the ninety and nine upon the mountains, and go seek that one which is gone astray. And when thou hast found it, bear it upon thy shoulders, rejoicing because thou hast found that which was gone astray; and bring it and let it mix with the flock.' (cf. Mt. 18:12–14; Lk. 15:4–7) So be thou also obedient, O bishop, and search out him that is lost, and seek him that is gone astray, and bring back him that is holding aloof. (cf. Ezk. 34:16) For thou hast authority *to forgive sins to him that offendeth;* (Lk. 4:18; Isa. 58:6) for thou hast put on the person of Christ. Wherefore our Saviour also said to him that had sinned: *Thy sins are forgiven thee: thy faith hath saved thee alive: go in peace.* (Mt. 9:2, etc.) Now 'peace' is the Church of tranquillity and rest, into which He restored those whom He loosed from sins, sound and without blemish, having a good hope and earnest in exercises of labours and afflictions (Mk. 10:52; Lk. 17:19; Mk. 5:34; Lk. 7:50; 8:48). For as a wise and compassionate physician He was healing all, and especially those who were gone astray in their sins; for *they that are whole have no need of a physician, but they that are sick.* (Mt. 9:12, etc.) And thou also, O bishop, art made the physician of the Church: do not therefore withhold the cure whereby thou mayest heal them that are sick with sins, but by all means cure and heal, and restore them sound to the Church. And be not reproached with this word which the Lord spoke: *With force and with derision ye were subduing them.* (Ezk. 34:4) Do not then use force, and be not violent, and pass not sentence sharply, and be not unmerciful; and deride not the people that is under thy charge, nor hide from them the word of repentance. For this is that, *With force and with derision ye were subduing them,* if thou deal harshly with thy lay folk, and correct them *with force,* and thrust and drive out and receive not back them that sin, but harshly and without mercy hide away repentance from them, and become a helper for the return of evil, and for the scattering of the flock *for meat to the beasts of the field,* (Ezk. 34:5) that is, to evil men of this world: nay, not to men in truth, but to beasts, to the heathen and to heretics. For to him who goes forth from the Church they presently join themselves, and like evil beasts devour him as meat. And by reason of thy harshness, he who goes forth from the Church will either depart and enter among the heathen, or will be sunk in the heresies; and he will become an alien altogether, and will depart from the Church and from the hope of God, And of the perdition of that man thou wilt be guilty, because thou art ready to drive out and cast away them that sin, and when they have repented and been converted thou wilt not receive them again. And thou hast fallen under the condemnation of that word of the Lord which He spoke: *Their feet are swift to evil, and they hasten to shed blood. Affliction and misery are in their ways; and the way of peace they have not known.* (Isa. 59:7–8) Now *the way of peace* is our Saviour Himself, as He said: *Forgive ye* the sins of them that sin, *that to you also* your sins *may be forgiven: give, and it shall be given unto you*; (Lk. 6:37–38) which means: *Give* forgiveness of sins, that *you* also may receive forgiveness. And again He taught us that we should be constantly praying at all times and saying: *Forgive us our debts, as we also have forgiven our debtors*. (Mt. 6:12) But if thou forgive not them that sin, how shalt thou receive forgiveness? Lo, is not thine own mouth against thee, and dost not thou condemn thyself in that thou hast said, 'I have forgiven,' when thou hast not forgiven, but in sooth hast slain? For he who drives a man out of the Church without mercy, what does he else but cruelly slay and shed blood without pity? For if by any a righteous man is unjustly slain with the sword, with God he shall be received into rest; (Wis. 4:7) but he who drives a man out of the Church and receives him not again, has committed everlasting murder, evilly and bitterly, and God gives for food to the grievous fire eternal him that is driven out from the Church, and regards not the mercy of God, and remembers not His goodness towards penitents, and takes not the example of Christ, nor considers those who repented of their many transgressions and received of Him forgiveness.

It behoves thee then, O bishop, to have before thine eyes those things which happened of old time, that from them thou mayest learn by comparison the healing of souls, and the admonition and reproof and exhortation of them that repent and have need of exhortation. And when thou judgest any persons, do thou with diligence and much investigation compare and follow out God's will: and as He did, so ought you also to do in your judgements. Hear then, O bishops, in regard to these things an apt and helpful example. It is written in the fourth Book of Kingdoms, and likewise in the second Book of Chronicles, thus: [1]*In those days reigned Manasseh, being twelve years old; and fifty years he reigned in Jerusalem: and the name of his mother was Hephzibah.* [2]*And he did that which was evil before the Lord, after the uncleanness of those peoples which the Lord destroyed from before the children of Israel.* [3]*And he turned again and built the shrines which Hezekiah his father had thrown down; and he set up pillars to Baal, and made abominations, as Ahab king of Israel had done. And he made altars for all the service of heaven, and worshipped all the hosts of heaven.* [4]*And he built altars to demons in the house of the Lord, whereof the Lord had said: In the house of the Lord in Jerusalem, there* will *I set my name. And Manasseh served the shrines, and said: My name shall endure for ever.* [5]*And he built altars for all the service of heaven in the two courts of the house of the Lord;* [6]*and he made his sons to pass through the fire in the valley of Bar-Hinnom. And he practised augury and used magic; and he made soothsayers and enchanters and diviners, and did much evil before the eyes of the Lord to provoke him to anger.* [7]*And he set the molten and graven image of abomination, which he had made, in the house of the Lord, whereof the Lord had said to David and to Solomon his son: In this house and in Jerusalem, which I have*

chosen out of all the tribes of Israel, will I set my name for
ever; [8]and I will no more withhold my feet from the land
of Israel, which I gave to their fathers: yet only if they will
keep all that I have commanded them, according to all
the commandments which my servant Moses commanded
them. [9]And they hearkened not: and Manasseh seduced
them to do that which was evil before the eyes of the Lord,
after the works of those peoples which the Lord destroyed
from before the children of Israel. [10]And the Lord spake
against Manasseh and against his people by the hand of
his servants the prophets, and said: [11]Because Manasseh
king of Judah hath done these evil abominations, as did
the Amorites which were before him, and hath made Ju-
dah also to sin with his idols: [12]therefore, thus saith the
Lord the God of Israel: Behold, I bring such evils upon
Jerusalem and upon Judah that everyone that heareth of
them, both his ears shalt tingle. [13]And I will stretch over
Jerusalem the measuring line of Samaria and the plum-
met of the house of Ahab; and I will wipe Jerusalem as
a water-pot is wiped, when it is overturned and falleth
upon its face. [14]And I wilt give the residue of mine inher-
itance to the sword, and wilt deliver them into the hand
of their enemies; and they shall be for a prey and a spoil
to all them that hate them, [15]because they have done evil
before mine eyes: for they are a provoking people, from the

day that I brought out their fathers from Egypt even unto this day. [16]*Moreover Manasseh shed much innocent blood, till he had filled Jerusalem from one end to the other with slain: by reason of the sins which he sinned, and caused Judah also to sin, in doing that which was evil before the Lord* (2 Ki. 21:1–16; cf. 2 Chr. 33:1–13). *And the Lord brought against them the chieftains of Assyria; and they took Manasseh and fettered him and cast ropes about him, and led him away to Babylon, and shut him up in prison all bound and fettered with iron* (cf. 2 Chr. 33:11) *And there was given him bran-bread by weight, and water mingled with gall in small measure, that he might be alive and be sore afflicted and vexed. And when he was afflicted exceeding much, he entreated the face of the Lord his God, and humbled himself exceedingly before the God of his fathers; and he prayed before the Lord God* (2 Chr. 33:12–13a) *and said:*

The Prayer of Manasseh:

[1]*O Lord God of my fathers, the God of Abraham and of Isaac and of Jacob and of their righteous seed,* [2]*who madest the heaven and the earth with all the adornment thereof;* [3]*who didst bind the sea and fix it by the com-*

mandment of thy word; who didst shut up the abyss and
seal it with thy fearful and glorious name; 4 *before whose*
power all things fear and tremble: 5 *for unsupportable is*
the exceeding beauty of thy glory, and none can endure to
stand before thine anger and thy wrath against sinners:
6 *without bound and without measure are the mercies of*
thy promises; 7 *for thou art a Lord long-suffering and mer-*
ciful and very gracious, and dost repent thee of the evil of
men. 8 *And thou, O Lord, according to the gentleness of*
thy goodness hast promised forgiveness to them that repent
of their sins, and in the multitude of thy mercies hast ap-
pointed repentance for the salvation of sinners. If then, O
Lord God of the righteous, thou didst not appoint repen-
tance to the righteous, to Abraham and to Isaac and to
Jacob: for neither did they sin against thee: yet hast thou
appointed repentance to me a sinner. 9 *For more than the*
sands of the sea are my sins multiplied, and I have no
respite to lift up my head for the multitude of mine in-
iquities. And now, O Lord, behold, I am justly afflicted;
and as I am worthy, so am I vexed. 10 *For lo, I am bound*
and bowed down with these many bands of iron, so that I
may not lift up my head: for neither am I worthy to lift up
mine eyes and behold and see the height of heaven, by rea-
son of the exceeding malice of my wickedness. For I have
done evil before thee, and provoked thy wrath, and have

set up idols and multiplied abominations. [11]*And now, behold, I bend the knees of my heart before thee, and beseech thy kindness:* [12]*I have sinned, O Lord, I have sinned; and because that I know my sins,* [13]*I make supplication before thee. Forgive me, O Lord, and destroy me not with mine offences, and be not angry with me for ever, nor keep against me mine evil deeds, neither condemn and cast me into the nether parts of the earth. For thou art the God of penitents:* [14] *wherefore in me also, O Lord, show thy goodness, that whereas I am unworthy, thou deliverest me after the multitude of thy mercies.* [15]*And for this will I praise thee ever and all the days of my life: for thee do all the hosts of heaven praise, and unto thee do they sing for evermore* (Pr. Man.1–15).

And the Lord hearkened to the voice of Manasseh, and had mercy on him (2 Chr. 33:13b). *And there was made over him a flame of fire, and all the iron bands that were upon him were melted and dissolved. And the Lord delivered Manasseh from his afflictions, and caused him to return to Jerusalem over his kingdom. And Manasseh knew the Lord, and said: He is the Lord God alone* (2 Chr. 33:13b). *And he served the Lord only, with all his heart and with all his soul, all the days of his life: and he was accounted righteous. And he slept with his fathers;*

and Amon his son reigned after him (2 Ki. 21:18; 2 Chr. 33.20).

You have heard, beloved children, how Manasseh served idols evilly and bitterly, and slew righteous men; yet when he repented God forgave him, albeit there is no sin worse than idolatry. Wherefore, there is granted a place for repentance. But concerning one who says: *I shall have good success when I shall walk in the perverse desire of my heart* (Dt. 29:19), thus saith the Lord: *I will stretch out my hand against him, and he shall be for a byword and a parable* (cf. Ezk. 14:9; Jer. 24:9; Dt. 28.37). For Amon also the son of Manasseh, when he conceived a design that he should transgress the Law, and said: *'My father from his youth did exceeding wickedly, and in his old age he repented: I also will walk in all the desires of my soul, and in the end will return to the Lord,' and did that which was evil before the Lord: he reigned but two years, because the Lord God quickly destroyed him from his good land* (cf. 2 Ki. 21:19–22). Beware therefore, you that are without faith, lest any man of you establish in his heart the thought of Amon, and perish suddenly and swiftly. Wherefore, O bishop, so far as thou canst, keep those that have not sinned, that they may continue without sinning; and those that repent of their sins heal and receive. But if thou receive not him who repents, because thou art without mercy, thou shalt sin against the Lord God; for thou obeyest not our Saviour and our God, to do as He also did with her that had sinned, whom the elders set before Him, and leaving the judgement in His hands, departed. But He, the Searcher of hearts, asked her and said to her: *Have the elders condemned thee, my daughter? She saith to him: Nay, Lord. And he said unto her: Go thy way: neither do I condemn thee* (cf. Jn 8:3–11). In Him therefore, our Saviour and King and God, be your pattern, O bishops, and do you imitate Him, that you may be quiet and meek, and merciful and compassionate, and peacemakers, and without anger, and teachers and correctors and receivers and exhorters; and that you be *not wrathful, nor tyrannical* (Tt. 1:7; cf. 1 Tim. 3:3); and that you be not insolent, nor haughty, nor boastful.

Chapter VIII

Warnings to Bishops; how they ought to conduct themselves.

You shall *not be lovers of wine* (1Tim. 3:2; Tt. 1:7), nor drunken; and you shall not be extravagant, nor luxurious, nor spending money improperly. You shall make use of the gifts of God not as alien funds, but as your own, *as* being appointed *good stewards* (cf. 1 Pt. 4:10) of God, who is ready to require at your hands an account of the discharge of the stewardship entrusted to you. Let that suffice you therefore which is enough for you, food and clothing and whatsoever is necessary. And you shall not make use of the revenues of the Church improperly, as alien funds, but with moderation; and you shall not procure pleasure and luxury from the revenues of the Church: *for sufficient for the labourer is his clothing and his food* (cf. Mt. 10:10; Lk. 10:7; 1 Tim. 5:18). *As good stewards of God* (cf. 1 Pt. 4:10), therefore, dispense well, according to the command, those things that are given and accrue to the Church, to orphans and widows and to those who are in distress and to strangers, as knowing that you have God who will require an account at your hands, who delivered this stewardship unto you. Divide and give therefore to all who are in want.

But be you also nourished and live from the revenues of the Church; yet do not devour them by yourselves, but let them that are in want be partakers with you, and you shall be without offence with God. For God upbraids those bishops who greedily and by themselves make use of the revenues of the Church, and make not the poor to be partakers with them, saying thus: *The milk ye eat, and with the wool ye are clothed* (Ezk. 34:3). For the bishops ought to be nourished from the revenues of the Church, but not to devour them; for it is written: *Thou shalt not muzzle the ox that treadeth out the corn* (Dt. 25:4 (1 Cor. 9:9; 1 Tim. 5:18)). As then the ox which works unmuzzled in the threshing floor eats, indeed, but does not consume the whole, so do you also, who work in the threshing floor which is the Church of God, be nourished from the Church, after the manner of the Levites who ministered in the tabernacle of witness, which in all things was a type of the Church: for even by its name it declares this, for the tabernacle 'of witness' foreshowed the Church. Now the Levites who ministered therein were nourished from those things which were given as offerings to God by all the people — gifts, and part-offerings, and first fruits, and tithes, and sacrifices, and offerings, and holocausts — without restraint, they and their wives and their sons and their daughters; because their work was the ministry of the tabernacle alone; and therefore they received no inheritance of land among the children of Israel, because the inheritance of Levi and his tribe was the produce of the people.

You also then to-day, O bishops, are priests to your people, and the Levites who minister to the tabernacle of God, the holy Catholic Church, who stand continually before the Lord God. You then are to your people priests and prophets, and princes and leaders and kings, and mediators between God and His faithful, and receivers of the word, and preachers and proclaimers thereof, and knowers of the Scriptures and of the utterances of God, and witnesses of His will, who bear the sins of all, and are to give an answer for all. You are they who have heard how the word sternly threatens you if you neglect and preach not God's will, who are in sore peril of destruction if you neglect your people. You again are they to whom is promised from God the great reward which is not falsified nor withheld, and grace unspeakable in great glory, when you shall minister well to the tabernacle of God, His Catholic Church. As then you have undertaken the burden of all, so also ought you to receive from all your people the ministration of food and clothing, and of other things needful. And so again, from these same gifts that are given you by the people which is under your charge, do you nourish the deacons and widows and orphans, and those who are in want, and strangers. For it behoves thee, O bishop, as a faithful steward to care for all; for as thou bearest the sins of all those under thy charge, so shalt thou beyond all men receive more abundant glory of God. For thou art an imitator of Christ: and as He took upon Him the sins of us all (cf. 1 Pt. 2:24), so it behoves thee also to bear the sins of all those under thy charge; for it is written in Isaiah concerning our Saviour thus: *We saw him having no splendour nor beauty, but as one whose aspect was marred and dejected beyond that of men; and as a man that suffereth, and knoweth to bear infirmities. For his face was changed: he was despised, and was nothing accounted in our eyes. But he endured our sins, and for our sake did sigh. But we accounted him as one smitten and plagued and brought low. Yet for our sins was he smitten, and, was made sick for our iniquities: and by his stripes all we are healed* (Isa. 53:2–5). And again He saith: *He bare the sins of many, and for their iniquity was delivered up* (Isa. 53:12). And in David and in all the prophets, and in the Gospel also, our Saviour makes intercession for our sins, whereas He is without sin. Therefore, as you have Christ for a pattern, so be you also a pattern to the people under your charge; and as He took upon Him our sins, so do you also take upon you the sins of the people. For you are not to think that the burden of the bishopric is light or easy. Wherefore, as you have taken up the burden of all, so the fruits also which you receive from all the people shall be yours, for all things of which you have need. And do you nourish well them that are in want, as being to render an account to Him who will require it, who can make no mistake nor be evaded. For as you administer the office of the bishopric, so from the same office of the bishopric ought you to be nourished, as the priests and Levites and ministers who serve before God, according as it is written in the Book of Numbers: [1] *The Lord spake with Aaron and said: Thou and thy sons and thy father's house shall take upon you the sins of the sanctuary; and thou and thy sons shall take upon you the sins of your priesthood.* [2] *And thy brethren the sons of thy father, the tribe of Levi, bring nigh unto thee, and let them be added to thee and minister unto thee. [3]And thou and thy sons with thee shall minister before this tabernacle of witness. Howbeit the sons of Levi shall not come nigh unto the vessels of the sanctuary and unto the altar, lest they die, they and you; [4]but let them be added unto thee, and let them keep the charges of the tabernacle of witness, according to all the ministry of the tabernacle: and a stranger shall not come nigh unto thee. [5]And ye shall keep the charges of the sanctuary and the charges of the altar: and there shall be no wrath against the children of Israel. [6]And I, behold, I have taken your brethren the sons of Levi from among the children of Israel: as a gift they are given unto the Lord, that they may perform the ministry of the tabernacle of witness. [7]And do thou and thy sons with thee keep your priesthood, according to all the ministry of the altar and of that which is within the veil; and perform your ministry as that which is given to your priesthood. But the stranger that cometh near shall die the death. [8]And the Lord spake with Aaron and said: Behold, I have given to you the charges of the first fruits, of every thing which is hallowed unto me by the children of Israel: to thee have I given them for a ministry, and to thy children after thee: it is an everlasting ordinance. [9]And this shall be yours, of every holy thing which is hallowed of their fruits and of*

*their offerings, and of all their sacrifices, and of all their
trespass offerings, and of all their sin offerings: all that they
shall offer to me of things hallowed shall be for thee and for
thy sons. [10]In the holy place ye shall eat thereof: every male
of you shall eat thereof, thou and thy sons: it shall be for
thee a holy thing. [11]And these shall be for thee the first
fruits of their gifts, of all the part-offerings of the children
of Israel: to thee have I given them, and to thy sons and thy
daughters with thee: it is an everlasting ordinance: every
one that is clean in thy house shall eat thereof. [12]All the
first fruits of oil, and all the first fruits of wine, and the
first fruits of corn, even all things that they shall give to the
Lord, shall be thine: [13]everyone that is clean in thy house
shall eat thereof. [14]And every devoted thing of the children
of Israel shall be thine; [15]and all that openeth the womb of
all flesh, even all which they offer to the Lord, from men
even unto beasts, shall be thine. Howbeit the firstborn of
men and the firstlings of unclean beasts which shall be offered, shall be redeemed. [16]And the redemption of them
shall be on this wise: from a month old and upward thou
shalt redeem with a price, five shekels according to the
shekel of the sanctuary, which are twenty shekels of silver.
[17]But the firstlings of oxen, and the firstlings of sheep and
of goats, thou shalt not redeem: they are holy: their blood
thou shalt pour out before the altar, and the fat of them*

*thou shalt offer up for an offering of a sweet savour unto
the Lord; [18]and their flesh shall be clean to thee. And the
top of the breast of the part-offering, and the right shoulder
shall be thine. [19]All part-offerings of the sanctuary, which
the children of Israel shall set apart unto the Lord, to thee
have I given them and to thy sons and to thy daughters
with thee: an ordinance for ever and an everlasting covenant is it before the Lord unto thee and unto thy seed after
thee. [20]And the Lord spake with Aaron and said: In their
land thou shalt receive no inheritance, and thou shalt have
no portion among them; for I am thy portion and thine
inheritance among the children of Israel. [21]And to the sons
of Levi, behold, I have given all the tithes of the children
of Israel for an inheritance, in return for their ministry
which they minister in the tabernacle of witness. [22]And the
children of Israel shall no more come nigh to the tabernacle
of witness, lest they contract a sin of death; [23]but the Levites shall perform the ministry of the tabernacle of witness,
and they shall take upon them their sins: it is an everlasting ordinance unto their generations. And among the children of Israel they shall receive no inheritance; [24]because
the tithes of the children of Israel, even all that they shall
set apart as part-offerings to the Lord, I have given to the
Levites for an inheritance. For which cause I said unto
them: Among the children of Israel they shall receive no*

inheritance. 25 *And the Lord spake with Moses and said
unto him:* 26 *Speak to the Levites and say to them: When ye
receive of the children of Israel the tithes which I have
given you from them for an inheritance, set by thereof, ye
also, a part-offering unto the Lord, a tithe of the tithes:*
27 *and your part-offering shall be accounted unto you as the
corn from the threshing floor, and as the part-offering of
the winepress.* 28 *So shall ye set apart, ye also, a part-
offering unto the Lord of all your tithes which ye receive
from all the children of Israel; and ye shall give thereof a
part-offering for the Lord unto Aaron the priest.* 29 *Of all
your gifts ye shall set by a part-offering unto the Lord, even
of the first fruits, part whereof he halloweth unto himself.*
30 *And say thou unto them: When ye have set apart his first
fruits therefrom, it shall be reckoned unto the Levites as
the produce of the threshing floor and as the produce of the
winepress:* 31 *and do ye eat thereof in every place, ye and
your households, because it is your reward in return for
your ministry in the tabernacle of witness:* 32 *and ye shall
contract no sin by reason thereof, when ye shall set apart
the first fruits thereof. And the holy things of the children
of Israel ye shall not profane, lest ye die* (Num. 18:1–32).

Chapter IX

An admonition to the People, that they should honour the Bishop.

Hear these things then, ye laymen also, the elect Church of God. For the former People also was called a church; but you are the Catholic Church, the holy and perfect, *a royal priesthood, a holy multitude, a people for inheritance* (1 Pt. 2:9; cf. Ex. 19:6), the great Church, the bride adorned for the Lord God (cf. Rev. 21:2; Isa. 61:10). Those things then which were said beforetime, hear thou also now. Set by part-offerings and tithes and first fruits to Christ, the true High Priest, and to His ministers, even tithes of salvation to Him the beginning of whose name is the Decade. Hear, thou Catholic Church of God, that wast delivered from the ten plagues, and didst receive the Ten Words, and didst learn the Law, and hold the faith, and know the Decade, and believe in the Yod in the beginning of the Name, and art established in the perfection of His glory: instead of the sacrifices which then were, offer now prayers and petitions and thanksgivings. Then were first fruits and tithes and part-offerings and gifts; but to-day the oblations which are offered through the bishops to the Lord God. For they are your high priests (cf. Did. 13:3); but the priests and Levites now are the presbyters and deacons, and the orphans and widows: but the Levite and high priest is the bishop. He is minister of the word and mediator; but to you a teacher, and your father after God, who begot you through the water. This is your chief and your leader, and he is your mighty king. He rules in the place of the Almighty: but let him be honoured by you as God, for the bishop sits for you in the place of God Almighty. But the deacon stands in the place of Christ; and do you love him. And the deaconess shall be honoured by you in the place of the Holy Spirit; and the presbyters shall be to you in the likeness of the Apostles; and the orphans and widows shall be reckoned by you in the likeness of the altar. And as it was not lawful for a stranger, that is for one who was not a Levite, to draw near to the altar or to offer aught without the high priest, so you also shall do nothing without the bishop. But if any man do aught without the bishop, he does it in vain, for it shall not be accounted to him for a work; for it is not fitting that any man should do aught apart from the high priest.

Do you therefore present your offerings to the bishop, either you yourselves, or through the deacons; and when he has received he will distribute them justly. For the bishop is well acquainted of those who are in distress, and dispenses and gives to each one as is fitting for him; so that one may not receive often in the same day or in the same week, and another receive not even a little. For whom the priest and steward of God knows to be the more in distress, him he succours according as he requires. And to those who invite widows to suppers let him send frequently her whom he knows to be in the more distress. (And again, if anyone gives bounties to widows, let him send her the rather who is in want.) But let the portion of the pastor be separated and set apart for him according to rule at the suppers or the bounties, even though he be not present, in honour of Almighty God. But how much soever is given to one of the widows, let the double be given to each of the deacons in honour of Christ, but twice twofold to the leader for the glory of the Almighty. But if anyone wish to honour the presbyters also, let him give them a double portion, as to the deacons; for they ought to be honoured as the Apostles, and as the counsellors of the bishop, and as the crown of the Church; for they are the moderators and councillors of the Church. But if there be also a lector, let him too receive with the presbyters. To every order, therefore, let everyone of the laity pay the honour which is befitting him, with gifts and presents and with the respect due to his worldly condition.

But let them have very free access to the deacons, and let them not be troubling the head at all times, but making known what they require through the ministers, that is through the deacons. For neither can any man approach the Lord God Almighty except through Christ. All things therefore that they desire to do, let them make known to the bishop through the deacons, and then do them. For neither formerly in the temple of the sanctuary was anything offered or done without the priest. And moreover, even the idol-temples of the impure and abhorred and reprobate heathen to this day imitate the sanctuary. Far indeed in comparison be the house of abomination from the sanctuary: nevertheless, even in their absurd rites they neither offer nor do anything without their unclean priest; but so they imagine, that the unclean priest is the mouthpiece of the stones; and they wait for what he will command them to do. And in all that they purpose to do they consult their unclean priest, and without him do nothing, And because they imagine that what they do is acceptable, they honour him and worship him, as it were for the honour of the dumb stones that are fixed in the walls, and for the service of the foul and evil and cruel demons. If then those who are vain, and their customs false, and who have no hope, but are deceived by an empty hope, study and desire to imitate the sanctuary, and bestow all honour upon those who stand before their absurd idols: you who manifestly and openly believe in the truth, and hold fast to the hope that is not belied, and wait for the glorious promise which shall never pass away nor be made void — why should not you rather honour the Lord God through those who preside over you?

Do you therefore esteem the bishop as the mouth of God. For if Aaron, because he interpreted to Pharaoh the words which were given through Moses, was called a prophet, as the Lord said to Moses: *Behold, I have given thee as a god to pharaoh and Aaron thy brother shall be to thee a prophet* (Ex. 7:1): why then should not you also reckon them as prophets who are for you the mediators of the word, and worship them as God? But for us now, Aaron is the deacon, and Moses is the bishop. Now if Moses was called a god by the Lord, let the bishop also be honoured by you as God, and the deacon as a prophet. Wherefore, for the honour of the bishop, make known to him all things that you do, and let them be performed through him. And if thou know of one who is in much distress, and the bishop know not of him, do thou inform him; and without him do not, to his discredit, anything, lest thou bring a reproach upon him as one who neglects the poor. For he who sets abroad an evil report against the bishop, whether by word or by deed, sins against God Almighty. And again, if any man speaks evil of a deacon, whether by word or deed, he offends against Christ, Wherefore in the Law also it is written: *Thou shalt not revile thy gods; and thou shalt not speak evil of a prince of thy people* (Ex. 22:28). Now let no man think that the Lord speaks here of idols of stone; but he calls 'gods' those who preside over you. Moses also saith in the Book of Numbers, when the people had murmured against him and against Aaron: *Not against us do ye murmur, but against the Lord God* (Ex. 16:8; cf. Num. 14:2). And our Saviour likewise said: *Everyone that rejecteth you, rejecteth me, and him that sent me* (Lk. 10:16). For what hope at all is there for him who speaks evil of the bishop, or of the deacon? For if one call a layman *fool,* or *raca, he is liable to the assembly* (Mt. 5:22), as one of those who rise up against Christ: because that he calls 'empty' his brother in whom Christ dwells, who is not empty but fulfilled; or calls him 'fool' in whom dwells the Holy Spirit of God, fulfilled with all wisdom: as though he should become a fool by the very Spirit that dwells in him! If then one who should say any of these things to a layman is found to fall under so great condemnation, how much more if he should dare to say aught against the deacon, or against the bishop, through whom the Lord gave you the Holy Spirit, and through whom you have learned the word and have known God, and through whom you have been known of God (cf. Gal 4.9), and through whom you were sealed (cf. Eph. 1:13; 4:30), and through whom you became sons of the light (cf. Jn. 12:36; 1 Th. 5:5), and through whom the Lord in baptism, by the imposition of hand of the bishop, bore witness to each one of you and uttered His holy voice, saying: *Thou art my son: this day have begotten thee* (Ps. 2:7 (Lk. 3:22)).

Wherefore, O man, know thy bishops, through whom thou wast made a son of God, and the right hand, thy mother; and love him who is become, after God, thy father and thy mother: for *whosoever shall revile his father or his mother, shall die the death* (Ex.

21:17; Mt. 15:4). But do you honour the bishops, who have loosed you from sins, who by the water regenerated you, who filled you with the Holy Spirit, who reared you with the word as with milk, who bred you up with doctrine, who confirmed you with admonition, and made you to partake of the holy Eucharist of God, and made you partakers and joint heirs of the promise of God. These reverence, and honour them with all honour; for they have received from God the authority of life and death: not as judging those who sin and condemning them to death in fire everlasting, by cutting off and casting away those who are judged, which God forbid, but that they may receive and save alive those who return and repent.

Let them be your rulers therefore, and let them be accounted of by you as kings; and do you offer them tribute in service as to kings; for by you they ought to be sustained, and those who are with them: for thus is it written in the first Book of Kingdoms: [10]*Samuel spake all the words of the Lord unto the people, which had asked of him a king,* [11]*and said to them: This is the law of the king that shall reign over you: your sons he will take, and will set them upon his chariots; and he will make of them runners before him,* [12]*and will make him captains of*

*thousands and captains of hundreds. And they shall reap
his harvest, and gather his vintage, and fashion the instru-
ments of his chariots.* 13 *And your daughters he will take
to be weavers, and to be the ministers of his house.* 14 *And
your fields, and your vineyards, and your oliveyards, even
the best of them, he will take away and give to his servants.*
15 *And he will take the tenth of your seed and of your vineyards, and give to his servants and to his eunuchs.* 16 *And
your servants and your handmaids, and the best of your
cattle, and your asses, he will take and tithe for the service
of his work*; 17 *and he will take the tenth of your sheep: and
ye also shall be his servants* (1 Sam. 8:10–17). Now in like case is also the bishop. For if the king who reigned over so numerous a people — as it is written in Hosea: *The people of the children of Israel was numerous as the sand which is upon the seashore, which may not be measured nor numbered* (Hos. 1:10) — took also from the people the ministrations which he required according to the multitude of that people: so now does the bishop also take for himself from the people those whom he accounts and knows to be worthy of him and of his office, and appoints him presbyters as counsellors and assessors, and deacons and subdeacons, as many as he has need of in proportion to the ministry of the house. And what can we say more? For the king who wears the

diadem reigns over the body alone, and binds and looses it but on earth; but the bishop reigns over soul and body, to bind and to loose on earth with heavenly power (cf. Mt. 16:19; 28:18). For great power, heavenly, almighty, is given to him. Therefore love the bishop as a father, and fear him as a king, and honour him as God. Your fruits and the works of your hands present to him, that you may be blessed; your firstfruits and your tithes and your vows and your part-offerings give to him; for he has need of them that he may be sustained, and that he may dispense also to those who are in want, to each as is just for him. And so shall thine offering be acceptable to the Lord thy God for a sweet savour, in the heights of heaven before the Lord thy God; and He will bless thee and multiply for thee the good things of His promise. For it is written in Wisdom: *Every simple soul shall be blessed: and a blessing shall be upon the head of him that giveth* (Prov. 11:25a, 26b LXX).

Wherefore be constantly doing work, and be labouring and offering an oblation. For the Lord has lightened the weight from you, and has loosed from you the collar-bands, and lifted from you the yoke of burden; and He has put away from you the Second Legislation after the abundance of His mercy; as it is written in Isaiah: *Say to them that are in bonds, Go forth* (Isa. 49:9)*;* and again: *To bring forth the prisoners from bonds* (Isa. 42:7). And in David he said: *His prisoners he hath not despised* (Ps. 69:33 (68:34 LXX)). And likewise in the Gospel He said: *Come unto me, all ye that toil and are laden with heavy burdens, and I will give you rest. Take my yoke upon you, and learn of me; for I am gentle and lowly in heart: and ye shalt find rest unto your souls. For my yoke is pleasant, and my burden is light* (Mt. 11:28–30).

If then the Lord, by the gift of His grace, has set you loose and given you rest, *and brought you out into refreshment* (Ps. 66:12 (65:12 LXX)), that you should no more be bound with sacrifices and oblations, and with sin offerings, and purifications, and vows, and gifts, and holocausts, and burnt offerings, and Sabbath idlings, and shewbread, and the observing of purifications; nor yet with tithes and firstfruits, and part-offerings, and gifts and oblations, — for it was laid upon them to give all these things as of necessity, but you are not bound by these things, — it behoves you to know the word of the Lord, who said: *Except your righteousness abound more than that of the scribes and Pharisees, ye shalt not enter into the kingdom of heaven* (Mt. 5:20). Now thus shall your righteousness abound more than their tithes and firstfruits and part-offerings, when you shall do as it is written: *Sell all thou hast, and give to the poor* (Mt. 19:21; cf. Lk. 12:33). So do, therefore, and keep the command through him who is bishop and priest and thy mediator with the Lord God. For thou art commanded to give, but he to dispense. And thou shalt require no account of the bishop, nor observe him, how he dispenses and discharges his stewardship, or when he gives, or to whom, or where, or whether well or ill, or whether he gives fairly; for he has One who will require, even the Lord God, who delivered this stewardship into his hands and held him worthy of the priesthood of so great an office. Wherefore, that thou observe not the bishop, nor require an account of him, nor speak ill of him and oppose God, nor offend the Lord, let that be set before thine eyes which is said to thee in Jeremiah: *Shall the clay say to the potter: Thou workest not, and hast not hands? as one who should say to his father or his mother: Why bearest thou me?* (Isa. 45:9–10) But do thou work and labour simply in the house of God; and let that saving word of the renewing of the Law be ever written and laid up in thy heart, and remember it, as the Lord said: *Thou shalt love the Lord thy God with all thy soul, and with all thy strength* (Mk. 12:30; Lk. 10:27

(Dt. 6:5)). Now *thy strength* is thy worldly substance. And not with the lips only shall you love the Lord, as did that People, to whom upbraiding them He saith: *This people honoureth me with their lips, but their heart is very far from me* (Isa. 29:13; Mt. 15:8)*;* but do thou love and honour the Lord *with all thy strength,* and offer His oblations ever at all times. And hold not aloof from the Church; but when thou hast received the Eucharist of the oblation, that which comes into thy hands cast in, that thou mayest share it with strangers: for this is collected and brought to the bishop for the entertainment of all strangers. Wherefore lay up and set by as much as thou canst, for the Lord has said in the Law: *Thou shalt not appear before me empty* (Ex. 23:15). Be doing good works therefore, and *laying up to thyself treasure* everlasting *in heaven, where the moth corrupteth not, neither do thieves steal* (Mt. 6:20; Lk. 12:33). And in so doing thou shalt not judge thy bishop nor thy fellow layman; for to you laymen it is said: *Judge not, that ye be not judged* (Mt. 7:1; Lk. 6:37). For if thou judge thy brother and condemn him, thou hast reckoned thy brother guilty: that is, thou hast condemned thyself; for thou shalt be judged with them that are guilty. For it is lawful for the bishops to judge, because to them it is said: *Be ye approved money-changers* (Agraphon): so that it behoves the bishop, as one who proves money, to separate the bad from the good, and to reject and cast away those that are altogether bad, and to leave in the melting-pot those that are hard, and for whatever reason faulty, like faulty coins. But to the layman it is not permitted to judge his neighbour, nor to lay upon himself a burden that is not his. For the weight of this burden is not for laymen, but for the bishop. Wherefore, being a layman, thou shalt not lay snares for thyself; but leave judgement in the hand of those who will have to render an account, and do thou study to work peace with all men; and love thy members, thy fellow laymen, for the Lord saith: *Love thy neighbour as thyself* (Mt. 19:19 (Lev. 19:18)).

Chapter X

Of False Brethren.

But if there be false brethren who, through envy or jealousy of the Enemy and Satan, who works in them, bring an accusation against any of the brethren falsely, or even truly, let them know that everyone who searches out such things for the purpose of accusing or slandering any man, is a son of wrath: and where wrath is, God is not; for wrath is of Satan, and through these false brethren he never suffers peace to be in the Church. Wherefore, when you have known those who are thus void of understanding, first of all believe them not; and secondly, do you the bishops and deacons be wary of them; and when you hear them saying anything against one of the brethren, take knowledge of him against whom they bring the accusation, and make inquiry prudently, and weigh his conduct; and if he is found blameworthy, do according to the teaching of our Lord which is written in the Gospel: *Reprove him between thyself and him; and save him when he repenteth and returneth. But if he be not persuaded, reprove him among two or three;* that that may be fulfilled which is said: *At the mouth of two or three witnesses every word shall be established* (Mt. 18:15–16 (cf. Lk. 17:3); Dt. 19:15). Now why, brethren, is it required that a testimony be established at the mouth of two or three witnesses? Because the Father and the Son and the Holy Spirit bear witness to the works of men. For where there is the admonition of doctrine, there also is correction and conversion of them that err. Wherefore, *at the mouth of two or three witnesses every word shall be established. But if he obey not, reprove him before the whole church. But if he obey not even the church, let him be accounted by thee as the heathen and as the publican* (Mt. 18:16–17). For the Lord has commanded you, O bishops, that you should not henceforth receive such a one into the Church as a Christian, nor communicate with him. For neither dost thou receive the evil heathen or publicans into the Church and communicate with them except they first repent, professing that they believe and henceforth will do no more evil works: for to this end did our Lord and Saviour grant a place for repentance to those who have sinned. For I Matthew also, who am one of the twelve Apostles who speak to you in this Didascalia, was formerly a publican; but now, because that I believed, I have obtained mercy, and have repented of my former deeds, and have been counted worthy also to be an apostle and preacher of the word. And the prophet John likewise preached in the Gospel to publicans; and he deprived them not of hope, but taught them how they should order themselves; and when they asked him for advice, he said to them: *Exact no more than that which is commanded and appointed you* (Lk. 3:13). And Zacchaeus, too, the Lord received unto repentance when he besought Him (cf. Lk. 19:1–10). Nor do we withhold life even from the heathen, if they will repent and put away and reject their error.

As a heathen, then, *and as a publican let him be accounted by you* (Mt. 18:17) who has been convicted of evil deeds and falsehood; and afterwards, if he promise to repent — even as when the heathen desire and promise to repent, and say 'We believe' we receive them into the congregation that they may hear the word, but do not communicate with them until they receive the seal and are fully initiated: so neither do we communicate with these until they show the fruits of repentance. But let them by all means come in, if they desire to hear the word, that they may not wholly perish; but let them not communicate in prayer, but go forth without. For they also, when they have seen that they do not communicate with the Church, will submit themselves, and repent of their former works, and strive to be received into the Church for prayer; and they likewise who see and hear them go forth like the heathen and publicans, will fear and take warning to themselves not to sin, lest it so happen to them also, and being convicted of sin or falsehood they be put forth from the Church. But thou shalt by no means forbid them to enter the Church and hear the word, O bishop; for neither did our Lord and Saviour utterly thrust away and reject publicans and sinners, but did even eat with them. And for this cause the Pharisees murmured against Him, and said: *He eateth with publicans and sinners.* Then did our Saviour make answer against their thoughts and their murmuring, and say: *They that are whole have no need of a physician, but they that are sick* (Mk. 2:16–17; Mt. 9:11–12; Lk. 5:30–31). Do you therefore consort with those who have been convicted of sins and are sick, and attach them to you, and be careful of them, and speak to them and comfort them, and keep hold of them and convert them. And afterwards, as each one of them repents and shows the fruits of repentance, receive him to prayer after the manner of a heathen. And as thou baptizest a heathen and then receivest him, so also lay hand upon this man, whilst all pray for him, and then bring him in and let him communicate with the Church. For the imposition of hand shall be to him in the place of baptism: for whether by the imposition of hand, or by baptism, they receive the communication of the Holy Spirit.

Wherefore, as a compassionate physician, heal all those who sin; and go about with all skill, and bring healing to bear for the succour of their lives. And thou shalt not be ready to cut off the members of the Church; but employ the bandages of the word, and the fomentations of admonition, and the compress of exhortation. But if the sore be sunken and lack flesh, nourish it and level it up with healing drugs; and if there be dirt in it, cleanse it with a pungent drug, that is with the word of rebuke. But if the flesh be over swollen, wear it down and level it with a violent drug, that is with the threat of judgement. But if gangrene should set in, cauterize it with burnings, that is, with incisions of much fasting cut away and clear out the rottenness of the sore. But if the gangrene assert itself and prevail even over the burnings, give judgement: and then, whichever member it be that is putrified, with advice and much consultation with other physicians, cut off that putrefied member, that it may not corrupt the whole body. Yet be not ready to amputate straightway, and be not in haste to have recourse at once to the saw of many teeth; but use first the knife and cut the sore, that it may be clearly seen, and that it may be known what is the cause of the disease that is hidden within; so that the whole body may be kept uninjured. But if thou see that a man will not repent, but has altogether abandoned himself, then with grief and to sorrow cut him off and cast him out of the Church. But if it be found that the hostile charge is false, and you the pastors, with the deacons, accept the falsehood as truth — whether through respect of persons, or by reason of the presents which you receive — and pervert judgement because you desire to do the will of the Evil One, and expel and cast out from the Church him that is accused, whereas he is innocent of this charge: you shall render an account in the day of the Lord; for it is written: *Thou shalt not respect persons in judgement* (Dt. 1:17)*;* and again the Scripture saith: *A bribe blindeth the eyes of them that see, and perverteth right words* (Ex. 23:8 (cf. Dt. 16:19)); and again it hath said: *Deliver ye the oppressed, and judge the fatherless, and acquit the widows* (Isa. 1:17); and: *Judge right judgement in the gates* (Zech. 8:16).

Give heed therefore that you be not respecters of persons and incur the judgement of the Lord's word, which He spoke thus: *Woe to them that make bitter sweet, and sweet bitter; and call light darkness, and darkness light; and acquit the wicked for his bribe, and turn away the innocency of the innocent* (Isa. 5:20, 23). But beware that you condemn not a man wrongfully, nor abet them that are evil; for when you judge others, you judge your own selves, as the Lord said: *With the judgement that ye judge, ye shall be judged; and as ye condemn, ye shall be condemned* (Mt. 7:2; cf. Lk. 6:37). Wherefore, remember and have ready by you this saying: *Forgive, and it shall be forgiven you; and condemn not, that ye may not be condemned* (Lk. 6:37 (cf. Mt. 6:14–15)).

But if your judgement be without respect of persons, O bishops, observe him that accuses his brother, whether he be not a false brother, and has brought the accusation out of envy or jealousy, that he may disturb the Church of God and slay him who is accused by him through his expulsion from the Church and his delivery over to the sword of fire. Judge him therefore, thou, sternly, because he has brought evil upon his brother. For as regards his own intent, if he had been able to catch beforehand the judge's ear, he would have slain his brother in fire. It is written: *Whoso sheddeth man's blood, his own blood shall be shed for the blood which he hath shed* (Gen. 9:6). If then he is found to be such, expel him from the Church with great denunciation as a murderer; and after a time, if he promise to repent, warn him and correct him sternly; and then lay hand upon him and receive him into the Church. And be wary and guard such a one, that he no more disturb any other. But if, after he is come in, you see that he is still contentious and minded to accuse others also, and mischievous and designing, and making false complaints against many: drive him out, that he may no further disturb and trouble the Church. For such a one, though he be within, yet because he is unseemly to the Church, he is superfluous to her, and there is no profit in him. For we see that there are some men born with superfluous members to their bodies, as fingers or other excessive flesh; but these, though they pertain to the body, are a reproach and a disgrace both to the body and to the man, because they are superfluous to him. Yet when they are removed by the surgeon, that man recovers the comeliness and beauty of his body; and he suffers no defect by the removal from it of that which was superfluous, but is even the more conspicuous in his beauty.

In like manner then do you also act, O pastors. For since the Church is a body, and the members are we who believe in God and abide in love in the fear of the Lord, even as we have received command to be perfect: therefore, one who contrives evil against the Church, and troubles her members, and loves the complaints and fault-findings of the Enemy, to wit, disturbances, quarrels, slanders, murmurings, contentions, controversies, accusations, charges, vexations: he that loves and does these things — rather it is the Enemy that works in him — and remains within the Church, the same is alien to the Church and a domestic of the Enemy; for to him he ministers that he may be working through him and may thwart and harass the Church. Such a one therefore, if he remain within, is a disgrace to the Church by reason of his blasphemies and his manifold disorder; for through him the Church of God comes in danger of being scattered. Deal with him therefore as it is written in Wisdom: *Put forth an evil man from the assembly, and his contention will go out with him; and make an end of strife and ignominy: lest, if he sit in the assembly, he dishonour you all* (Prov. 22:10). For when he has gone forth twice from the Church, he is justly cut off; and the Church is the more beautiful in her proper form, forasmuch as peace has been restored to her, which before was wanting to her: for from that hour the Church remains free from blasphemy and disorder. But if your mind be not pure — whether it be through respect of persons, or the gifts of filthy lucre which you receive — and you endure that an evil person should remain among you; or again, if you thrust away and expel from the Church them that are of good conversation, and foster among you many that are evil, contentious persons and scatterers of the flock and riotous: you will bring blasphemy upon the assembly of the Church, and will run the risk of scattering her through these persons; and you will have put yourselves in deadly peril of forfeiting eternal life — because you have pleased men, and have turned back from the truth of God, through respect of persons and the habit of receiving empty gifts: and you will have scattered the Catholic Church, the beloved daughter of the Lord God.

Chapter XI

An Exhortation to Bishops and Deacons.

Strive therefore, O bishops, together with the deacons, to be right with the Lord; for the Lord has said: *If ye will be right with me, I also will be right with you; and if ye will walk perversely with me, I also will walk perversely with you, saith the Lord of Hosts* (cf. Ps. 18:25–26; Lev. 26:23–24, 27–28). Be *right* therefore, that you may deserve to receive praise of the Lord, and not blame from him who is of the contrary part.

Let the bishops and the deacons, then, be of one mind; and do you shepherd the people diligently with one accord. For you ought both to be one body, father and son; for you are in the likeness of the Lordship. And let the deacon make known all things to the bishop, even as Christ to His Father. But what things he can, let the deacon order, and all the rest let the bishop judge. Yet let the deacon be the hearing of the bishop, and his mouth and his heart and his soul; for when you are both of one mind, through your agreement there will be peace also in the Church.

Now for a Christian this is becoming praise, that he have no evil word with any man. But if by the agency of the Enemy some temptation befall a man, and he have a lawsuit, let him strive to be quit of it, even though he be to suffer some loss: and at all events let him not go to the tribunals of the heathen. And you shall not admit a testimony from the heathen against any of our own people; for through the heathen the Enemy contrives against the servants of God. Wherefore, because the heathen are to stand on the left (cf. Mt. 25:33), He called them 'the left hand;' for our Saviour spoke thus to us: *Let not your left hand know what your right hand doeth* (Mt. 6:3). For the heathen are not to know of your lawsuits, and you shall not admit a testimony from them against yourselves, nor go to law before them (cf. 1 Cor. 6:1): as also in the Gospel He saith: *Give what is Caesar's to Caesar, and what is God's to God* (Mt. 22:21; Lk. 20:25). Be thou willing therefore to suffer a loss, and striving rather to make peace. For when thou shalt suffer any worldly loss for the sake of peace, with God it shall be gain to thee, because that thou fearest God and doest according to His commandment.

But if there be brethren who have a quarrel one with another — which God forbid — you the leaders should know forthwith that it is no work of brotherhood in the Lord that they perform who have dared so to do. But if one of them be found to be of the sons of God, being meek and yielding, he is a son of the light (cf. Jn. 12:36). But one who is hard and froward, and overreaching and blasphemous, is a hypocrite, and the Enemy works in him. Reprove him therefore, and rebuke and upbraid him, and put him forth for correction; and afterwards, as we have already said, receive him, that he may not utterly perish. For when such are corrected and reproved, you will not have many lawsuits. But if they know not the word which was spoken by our Lord in the Gospel, which saith: *How many times, if my brother offend against me, shall I forgive him?* (Mt. 18:21) but are angry one with another and become enemies, teach them, you, and reprove them, and make peace between them; for the Lord has said: *Blessed are the peacemakers* (Mt. 5:9). And know that it behoves the bishop and the presbyters to judge warily: as our Saviour said when we asked Him, *How many times, if my brother offend against me, shall I forgive him? unto seven times?* (Mt. 18:21) But our Lord taught us and said to us: *Not seven times, I say, only, but even unto seventyfold seven.* (Mt. 18:22) For so the Lord desires, that they who are His in truth should never have anything at all against any man, and should not be angry with any man: how much less does He desire that men should have lawsuits one with another. But if aught should happen to come about through the agency of the Enemy, so let them be judged before you as you also are surely to be judged.

First, then, let your judgements be held on the second day of the week, that if perchance anyone should contest the sentence of your words, you may have space until the Sabbath to compose the matter, and may make peace between them that are at odds and reconcile them on the Sunday. Now let the presbyters and the deacons be ever present in all judgements with the bishops. Judge without respect of persons.

When therefore the two parties who have the suit or quarrel one with another shall come and stand together in the judgement (cf. Dt. 19:17), as the Scripture saith, after you have heard them, pass sentence righteously. And give diligence to keep them in friendship before the sentence is pronounced upon them, lest there go forth from you against one of them, being a brother, a condemnation of earthly judgement. And so judge as you also are surely to be judged, even as you have Christ for partner and assessor and counsellor and spectator with you in the same cause. But if there be any who are accused by some one, it being charged against them that they conduct themselves not well in the way of the Lord: again, hearing both parties, make diligent inquiry, as being to give sentence in a matter of everlasting life or cruel and bitter death. For if a man is truly convicted, and he be condemned and go forth from the Church, he has been cast out from life and glory everlasting, and is become reprobate among men and guilty before God. Judge therefore, according to the magnitude of the charge, whatever it be, with much mercy; and incline rather to save alive without respect of persons than to destroy, by condemning, those who are judged.

But if there be one who is innocent, and he be condemned by the judges through respect of persons, the judgement of unjust judges shall do him no hurt with God, but shall rather profit him; for but for a little while is he unjustly judged by men, but afterwards, in the day of judgement, because he has been unjustly condemned, he shall be the judge of his unjust judges. For you have been the arbiters of an unjust judgement, and therefore shall be requited by God accordingly, and cast out of the Catholic Church of God. And that shall be fulfilled in your case: *With what judgement ye judge, ye shall be judged* (Mt. 7:2).

Wherefore, when you sit to judge, let both parties — for we do not call them brothers until peace has been made between them — come and stand together; and do you make prudent and diligent inquiry as between those who have the suit and quarrel one with another. And learn first concerning him who makes the accusation, whether there be any accusation against him also, or whether perchance he has brought charges against others as well; and again, whether he has brought his accusation out of any former enmity or quarrel, or out of envy; and inquire also of what manner his conversation is — whether he is meek, and without anger, and not given to slander, and whether he loves the widows and the poor and strangers, and is *not greedy of filthy lucre* (1 Tim. 3:8); and whether he is quiet, and friendly to all and a lover of all; whether he is merciful and open-handed to give, and not a glutton and greedy, nor grasping, nor drunken, nor intemperate, nor slothful: for *the perverse heart contriveth evil, and the same disturbeth cities at all times* (Prov. 6:14); and whether no such evil has been committed by him as is done in the world. And if he that makes the accusation is free from all these things, it is already evident and manifest that he is trustworthy, and that his accusation is true. But if he is known to be perverse and contentious, and his conduct not right, this also is evident, that he brings false witness against your brother. When therefore he is found and known to be an injurious person, rebuke him and put him forth for a time, until he repent and be converted and weep: lest perchance he again blaspheme against some other of our brethren who is of good conversation; or lest, while he sits in your congregation, some other like him, seeing him unreproved, should himself dare to do in like manner to one of our brethren, and should perish before God. But if he who has sinned is rebuked and corrected and put forth for a season, he also who was ready to imitate him and to do as he did, having seen him put forth, will fear lest it happen to him in like manner, and will submit himself: and he shall live before God, and in no wise be put to shame among men.

And concerning him again who is judged take counsel and thought among you in like manner: and observe his manners and conduct in the world, whether perchance you have heard many charges against him, or whether he has committed many crimes. For if he is found to have committed crimes, it is likely that this charge also which they prefer against him is true. But again, it may happen that he had formerly committed some sin, but is innocent of this present charge. Wherefore, make diligent investigation of these things, that you may give sentence with great caution and surety; and do you judge rightfully concerning him who is found to be guilty, and pass judgement upon him. But let anyone of them who will not abide by your judgement be reproved and put forth from the congregation until he repent and make entreaty of the bishop or of the Church, and confess that he has sinned, and is penitent. And thus shall advantage accrue to many: lest at any time some other, seeing him sit in the Church unrebuked and uncorrected, should himself dare to do as he did, thinking him alive among men, whereas with God he is lost. But if you hear one party alone, while the other is not present to make his defence to the charge which they bring against him, and you pass sentence hastily, without counsel and without inquiry, and, in accordance with the falsehoods which you have believed, condemn him while he is not present to defend himself: you shall be partners before God of him that brought the false witness, and with him *you* shall be punished by God. For the Lord has said in Proverbs: *He that meddleth in a quarrel that is not his own, is as he that taketh hold of a dog's tail* (Prov. 26:17); and again in another place He has said: *Judge right judgement;* and again He has said: *Judge the fatherless, and justify the widows* (cf. Dt. 1:16; Zech. 8:16 (cf. Jn. 7:24)); and again He saith: *Deliver the oppressed, and sever every bond of iniquity* (Isa. 1:17; 58:6). But if you resemble those elders who were in Babylon, who bore false witness against Susanna and wickedly condemned her to death (Dan. 13 LXX; Susanna), you also shall be partners of their judgement and of their condemnation; for the Lord by Daniel saved Susanna from the hand of the ungodly, and those elders who were guilty of her blood He condemned to fire.

Now very far apart do we set the things of the sanctuary from those of the world; nevertheless this we say: You see, brethren, how, when murderers are brought before the civil authority, the judges question diligently those who bring them, and learn from them what they have done. And then again they ask the criminal whether these things are so; and though he himself confess and say, 'Yea' they do not send him straightway to death, but question him again for many days, and drawing the curtain take thought and counsel much together. And then at length they pass upon him the sentence of death, and lifting up their hands to heaven protest that they are innocent of the man's blood. And these things they do though they are heathens and know not God nor the requital they receive from God for those whom they judge and condemn unjustly. And do you, who know who is our God and what His judgements, dare to give sentence upon one who is not guilty? We counsel you therefore that you make inquiry with diligence and much caution. For the word of sentence which you decree ascends straightway to God; and if you have justly judged, you shall receive of God the reward of justice, both now and hereafter; but if you have judged unjustly, again you shall receive of God a recompense accordingly. Strive therefore, brethren, that you be worthy to receive praise from God, and not blame; for praise from God is everlasting life to men, but blame from God is eternal death to men.

Have a care therefore, O bishops, that you be not in haste to sit in judgement forthwith, lest you be constrained to condemn a man; but before they come and stand in the judgement, admonish them and make peace between them. And admonish those who have the suit and quarrel one with another, and teach them in the first place that it is not right for any man to be angry, because the Lord has said: *Every one that is angry with his brother is liable to the judgement* (Mt. 5:22); and secondly, that if it should happen through the agency of the Enemy that some anger arise, they ought at once, that very day, to be reconciled and appeased, and to be at peace with one another. For it is written: *Let not the sun go down upon thine anger* (Eph. 4:26) against thy brother; and in David also He saith: *Be angry, and sin not* (Ps. 4:5; Eph. 4:26); that is, be speedily reconciled, lest, if anger continue, malice arise and beget sin. He saith in Proverbs: *The soul that keepeth malice shall die* (Prov. 12:28; cf. Herm. Vis. 2:3:1 (7:1)). And our Lord and Saviour also said: *If thou offer thy gift upon the altar, and there remember that thy brother keepeth any malice against thee, leave thy gift before the altar, and go, first be reconciled with thy brother: and then come, offer thy gift* (Mt. 5:23–24). Now the gift of God is our prayer and our Eucharist. If then thou keep any malice against thy brother, or he against thee, thy prayer is not heard and thy Eucharist is not accepted; and thou shalt be found void both of prayer and Eucharist by reason of the anger which thou keepest. A man ought to pray diligently at all times; but those who bear anger and malice towards their brethren God does not hear; and though thou pray three times in one hour, thou shalt gain nothing, for thou art not heard by reason of thine enmity against thy brother. Wherefore, if thou carest and strivest to be a Christian, follow the saying of the Lord which saith: *Loose all ties of iniquity; and sever the bands of violence and oppression* (Isa. 58:6). For upon thee has our Saviour laid this power, that thou shouldst forgive thy brother who has offended against thee *unto seventyfold seven time* (Mt. 18:22), that is, four hundred and ninety. How many times then hast thou forgiven thy brother, that thou wilt no more forgive him, but keepest malice and maintainest enmity, and desirest to go to law? Therefore is thy prayer hindered. But even if thou hast forgiven the full four hundred and ninety times, add still more for thine own sake, and of thy bounty, without anger, forgive thy brother. And if thou do it not for thy brother's sake, bethink thee and do it at least for thine own; and forgive thy neighbour, that thou mayest be heard when thou prayest, and mayest offer an acceptable oblation to the Lord.

Wherefore, O bishops, that your oblations and your prayers may be acceptable, when you stand in the Church to pray let the deacon say with a loud voice: 'Is there any man that keepeth aught against his fellow?' that if there be found any who have a lawsuit or quarrel one with another, thou mayest entreat them and make peace between them. They who enter a house and say, *Peace be in this house* (Mt. 10:12; Lk. 10:5), both are proclaimers of peace and do bring peace. If then thou preach peace to others, still more does it behove thee to have peace with thy brethren. As a son of light and peace therefore, be thou light and peace to all men; and contend with no man, but be in quiet and peace with all men. And be a helper with God that the number of those who are saved may be increased; for this is the will of the Lord God. But they who love enmity and quarrels, and contentions and lawsuits, are enemies of God. For the Lord from the beginning, through the prophets and righteous men, called all generations to repentance and salvation; and we, moreover, the Apostles, who have been accounted worthy to be the witnesses of His manifestation and preachers of His divine word, have heard from the mouth of the Lord Jesus Christ, and do know of a surety and say what is His will, and the will of His Father, *that no man should perish, but that all men should* believe and *be saved* (cf. 2 Pt. 3:9; 1Tim. 2:4). For this is that which He taught us to say when we pray: *Thy will be done in earth, as in heaven* (Mt. 6:10); that as the angels of heaven and the hosts and all His ministers praise God, so too on earth all men should praise God. It is His will, then, to save all; and this is His pleasure, that they who are saved should be many.

He who is contentious, or makes himself an enemy to his neighbour, diminishes the people of God. For either he drives out of the Church him whom he accuses, and diminishes her and deprives God of the soul of a man which was being saved, or by his contention he expels and ejects himself from the Church, and so again he sins against God. For God our Saviour spoke thus: *Everyone that is not with me, is against me; and everyone that gathereth not with me, scattereth* (Mt. 12:30). Wherefore thou art no helper with God for the gathering together of the people, because thou art a disturber and a scatterer of the flock, and an adversary and enemy of God. Be not therefore forever embroiled in contentions and quarrels, or wrangling, or enmity, or lawsuits, lest thou scatter some one from the Church. For we by the power of the Lord God have gathered men from all peoples and from all tongues, and have brought them to the Church with much labour and toil and in daily peril, that we might do the will of God and *fill the house with guests* (Mt. 22:10), that is His holy Catholic Church, that they might be glad and rejoicing, and be praising and glorifying God who called them to life.

Be you then, O laymen, peaceable one with another, and strive like wise doves to fill the Church, and to convert and tame those that are wild and bring them into her midst. And for this is the great reward that is promised by God: if you deliver them from fire, and present them to the Church firmly established and faithful.

CHAPTER XII

To Bishops: that they should be peaceable.

And you the bishops, be not hard, nor tyrannical, nor wrathful, and be not rough with the people of God which is delivered into your hands. And destroy not the Lord's house nor scatter His people; but convert all, that you may be helpers with God; and gather the faithful with much meekness and long-suffering and patience, and without anger, and with doctrine and exhortation, as ministers of the kingdom everlasting.

And in your congregations in the holy churches hold your assemblies with all decent order, and appoint the places for the brethren with care and gravity. And for the presbyters let there be assigned a place in the eastern part of the house; and let the bishop's throne be set in their midst, and let the presbyters sit with him. And again, let the lay men sit in another part of the house toward the east. For so it should be, that in the eastern part of the house the presbyters sit with the bishops, and next the lay men, and then the women that when you stand up to pray, the rulers may stand first, and after them the lay men, and then the women also. For it is required that you pray toward the east, as knowing that which is written: *Give ye glory to God, who rideth upon the heaven of heavens toward the east* (Ps. 67:34 LXX).

But of the deacons let one stand always by the oblations of the Eucharist; and let another stand without by the door and observe them that come in; and afterwards, when you offer, let them minister together in the Church. And if anyone be found sitting out of his place, let the deacon who is within reprove him and make him to rise up and sit in a place that is meet for him. For our Lord likened the Church to a fold; for as we see the dumb animals, oxen and sheep and goats, lie down and rise up, and feed and chew the cud, according to their families, and none of them separate itself from its kind; and see the wild beasts also severally range with their like upon the mountains: so likewise in the Church ought those who are young to sit apart, if there be room, and if not to stand up; and those who are advanced in years to sit apart. And let the children stand on one side, or let their fathers and mothers take them to them; and let them stand up. And let the young girls also sit apart; but if there be no room, let them stand up behind the women. And let the young women who are married and have children stand apart, and the aged women and widows sit apart. And let the deacon see that each of them on entering goes to his place, that no one may sit out of his place. And let the deacon also see that no one whispers, or falls asleep, or laughs, or makes signs. For so it should be, that with decency and decorum they watch in the Church, with ears attentive to the word of the Lord.

But if any brother or sister come from another congregation, let the deacon question her and learn whether she is married, or again whether she is a widow who is a believer; and whether she is a daughter of the Church, or belongs perchance to one of the heresies; and then let him conduct her and set her in a place that is suitable for her. But if a presbyter should come from another congregation, do you the presbyters receive him with fellowship into your place. And if it be a bishop, let him sit with the bishop; and let him accord him the honour of his rank, even as himself. And do thou, O bishop, invite him to discourse to thy people; for the exhortation and admonition of strangers is very profitable, especially as it is written: *There is no prophet that is acceptable in his own place* (Lk. 4:24). And when you offer the oblation, let him speak. But if he is wise and gives the honour to thee, and is unwilling to offer, at least let him speak over the cup. But if, as you are sitting, some one else should come, whether a man or a woman, who has some worldly honour, either of the same district or of another congregation: thou, O bishop, if thou art speaking the word of God, or hearing, or reading, shalt not respect persons and leave the ministry of thy word and appoint them a place; but do thou remain still as thou art and not interrupt thy word, and let the brethren themselves receive them. And if there be no place, let one of the brethren who is full of charity and loves his brethren, and is one fitted to do an honour, rise and give them place, and himself stand up. But if, while younger men or women sit, an older man or woman should rise and give up their place, do thou, O deacon, scan those who sit, and see which man or woman of them is younger than the rest, and make them stand up, and cause him to sit who had risen and given up his place; and him whom thou hast caused to stand up, lead away and make him to stand behind his neighbours: that others also may be trained and learn to give place to those more honourable than themselves. But if a poor man or woman should come (cf. Jas. 2:2), whether of the same district or of another congregation, and especially if they are stricken in years, and there be no place for such, do thou, O bishop, with all thy heart provide a place for them, even if thou have to sit upon the ground; that thou be not as one who respects the persons of men, but that thy ministry may be acceptable with God.

Chapter XIII

An Instruction to the People to be constant in assembling in the Church.

Now when thou teachest, command and warn the people to be constant in assembling in the Church, and not to withdraw themselves but always to assemble, lest any man diminish the Church by not assembling, and cause the body of Christ to be short of a member. For let not a man take thought of others only, but of himself as well, hearkening to that which our Lord said: *Everyone that gathereth not with me, scattereth* (Mt. 12:30). Since therefore you are the members of Christ, do not scatter yourselves from the Church by not assembling. Seeing that you have Christ for your head, as He promised — for you are partakers with us — be not then neglectful of yourselves, and deprive not our Saviour of His members, and do not rend and scatter His body. And make not your worldly affairs of more account than the word of God; but on the Lord's day leave every thing and run eagerly to your Church;

for she is your glory. Otherwise, what excuse have they before God who do not assemble on the Lord's day to hear the word of life and be nourished with the divine food which abides for ever? For you are eager to receive temporal things and those that are but for a day and an hour, but those that are eternal you neglect; and you are anxious about baths, and to be fed with the meat and drink of the belly, and about other things, but for the things eternal you have no care, but neglect your soul and have no zeal for the Church, to hear and receive the word of God. And in comparison of them that err what excuse have you? For the heathen, when they daily rise from their sleep, go in the morning to worship and minister to their idols; and before all their works and undertakings they go first and worship their idols. Neither at their festivals and their fairs are they wanting, but are constant in assembling: not only they who are of the district, but even those who come from afar; and all likewise assemble and come to the spectacle of their theatre. And so in like manner they who are vainly called Jews, they remain idle one day after six, and assemble in their synagogue; and never do they withdraw themselves or neglect their synagogue, nor disregard their days of idleness — even they who by reason of their unbelief are made void of the power of the word, and of the very name by which they call themselves Jews: for 'Jew' is interpreted 'confession' but these are no confessors, since they do not confess the passion of Christ, which by transgression of the Law they caused, that they should repent and be saved. If then they who are not saved bestow care at all times on things wherein there is no profit and which avail them nothing, what excuse has he before the Lord God who withdraws himself from the assembly of the Church, and does not even imitate the gentiles, but by reason of his non-attendance grows indifferent and careless, and stands aloof and does evil to whom the Lord said by Jeremiah: *My laws ye have not kept* (Ezk. 5:7)*: but neither have ye conversed after the laws of the gentiles; and ye have well nigh surpassed them in evildoing* (Ezk. 16:47); and: *Do the gentiles exchange their gods, which yet be no gods? But my people have exchanged their honour for that which is without profit* (Jer. 2:11). How then shall he excuse himself who is indifferent and has no zeal for the assembly of the Church? But if there be anyone who takes occasion of worldly business to withdraw himself, let him know this, that the trades of the faithful are called works of superfluity; for their true work is religion. Pursue your trades therefore as a work of superfluity, for your sustenance, but let your true work be religion.

Have a care therefore that you never withdraw yourselves from the assembly of the Church. But if any man leave the assembly of the Church of God and go to the assembly of the gentiles, what shall he say, and what excuse can he make to God in the day of judgement? Seeing that he has left the holy Church, and the words of the living God, which are living and life-giving and able to redeem and to deliver from fire and to save alive, and has gone to the assembly of the gentiles, because he has lusted after the spectacle of the theatre. Therefore shall he be accounted as one of them that go in thither; because he has lusted to hear and receive their fables, which are those of dead men and are from the spirit of Satan: for they are dead and deadly, and turn away from the faith and bring to everlasting fire. Nay, but the things of the world are your care, and you attend to the affairs of this life and scorn to betake yourselves to the Catholic Church, the beloved daughter of the Lord God Most High, that you may receive the teaching of God which endures for ever and is able to save them that receive the word of life.

Be constant therefore in coming together with the faithful who are being saved in your mother the Church, the living and life-giving.

And beware of assembling with them that are perishing in the theatre, which is the assembly of the heathen, of error and of destruction. For he who enters an assembly of the gentiles shall be accounted as one of them, and shall receive the Woe. For to such the Lord God said by Isaiah: *Woe, woe to them that come from the spectacle* (cf. Targ. Ps-Jon. on Dt. 28:19). And again He saith: *Ye women that come from the spectacle, come: for it is a people without understanding* (Isa. 27:11 LXX). 'Women' then, He called the Churches, which He called and redeemed and brought forth from the spectacle of the theatre, and took and received; and He taught us from henceforth to go thither no more. For He saith in Jeremiah: *Ye shall not learn according to the ways of the gentiles* (Jer. 10:2). And He saith again in the Gospel: *In the way of the gentiles ye shall not go; and into the cities of the Samaritans ye shall not enter* (Mt. 10:5). Here then He commands and warns us wholly to avoid all heresies, which are *the cities of the Samaritans;* and furthermore, that we should keep far away from the assemblies of the gentiles, and not enter strange congregations; and that we should utterly avoid the theatre, and their fairs which are held for the sake of idols. A believer must not even come near to a fair, except to buy him nourishment for body and soul. Therefore, avoid all vain shows of the idols, and the festivals of their fairs.

And let those who are young in the Church be ministering diligently, without sloth, in all things that are needful, with much reverence and modesty. Do you the faithful therefore, all of you, daily and hourly, whenever you are not in the Church, devote yourselves to your work; so that in all the conduct of your life you may either be occupied in the things of the Lord or engaged upon your work, and may never be idle. For the Lord has said: [6]*Imitate the ant, O sluggard, and emulate her ways, and be wiser than she.* [6]*For she hath no husbandry, nor any to compel her, nor is she under authority:* [8]*yet she gathereth her bread in summer, and storeth up for her much food in the harvest* (Prov. 6:6–8). And again He saith: [8a]*Go to the bee, and learn how she worketh. For her work she performeth in wisdom:* [8b]*and there is brought of her labour to be food for rich and poor. Beloved and praiseworthy is she:* [8c]*and albeit she is little in strength, she honoureth wisdom, and is commended there-*

by. [9]*How long wilt thou sleep, thou sluggard? When wilt thou arise from thy sleep?* [10]*Thou shalt slumber a little, and sleep a little, and sit a little, and lay thy hand upon thy bosom a little:* [11]*and poverty shall overtake thee as a runner, and want as a lusty man.* [11a]*But if thou wilt not be slothful, thine increase shall abound and overflow as a fountain; and poverty as a feeble runner shall depart from thee* (Prov. 6:8a–8c, 9–11a; cf. Sir. 11:3). Therefore, be always working, for idleness is a blot for which there is no cure. *But if any man among you will not work, let him not eat* (2 Th. 3:10): for the Lord God also hateth sluggards; for it is not possible for a sluggard to be a believer.

Chapter XIV

On the time for the appointment of Widows.

Appoint as a widow one that is not under fifty years old (1 Tim. 5:9), who in some sort, by reason of her years, shall be remote from the suspicion of taking a second husband. But if you appoint one who is young to the widows' order, and she endure not widowhood because of her youth, and marry, she will bring a reproach upon the glory of widowhood; and she shall render an account to God, first, because she has married a second husband; and again, because she promised to be a widow unto God, and was receiving alms as a widow, but did not continue in widowhood. But if there be one who is young, who has been a short time with her husband, and her husband die, or for any other cause there be a separation, and she continue by herself alone, having the honour of widowhood: she shall be blessed of God; for she is likened to the widow of Sarepta of Sidon with whom rested the holy angel, the prophet of God. Or again, she shall be like Anna, who hailed the coming of Christ and received a good testimony; and she shall be honoured for her virtue, winning honour on earth from men, and praise from God in heaven.

But let not young widows be appointed to the widows' order: yet let them be taken care of and helped, lest by reason of their being in want they be minded to marry a second time, and some harmful matter ensue. For this you know, that she who marries one husband may lawfully marry also a second; but she who goes beyond this is a harlot (cf. 1 Cor. 7:39; Rom. 7:2–3). Wherefore, assist those who are young, that they may persevere in chastity unto God. And do thou accordingly, O bishop, bestow care upon these. And be mindful also of the poor, and assist and support them, even though there be among them those who are not widowers or widows, yet are in need of help through want or sickness or the rearing of children, and are in distress. It behoves thee to be careful of all and heedful of all. And hence it is that they who give gifts do not themselves with their own hands give them to the widows, but bring them to thee, that thou who art well acquainted of those who are in distress mayest, like a good steward, make distribution to them of those things which are given to thee: for God knows who it is that gives, even though he does not chance to be present. And when thou makest distribution, tell them the name of him who gave, that they may pray for him by name. For in all the Scriptures the Lord makes mention of the poor, and gives command concerning them; and even if they be married persons. And he adds further by Isaiah and says thus: *Break thy bread to the hungry: and the poor man, that hath no roof, bring into thine house; and when thou seest the naked, cover him: and thou shalt not despise one that is of thine own flesh* (Isa. 58:7). By all means therefore be careful of the poor.

Chapter XV

How Widows ought to deport themselves.

Every widow therefore ought to be meek and quiet and gentle. And let her also be without malice and without anger; and let her not be talkative or clamorous, or forward in tongue, or quarrelsome. And when she sees anything unseemly done, or hears it, let her be as though she saw and heard it not. For a widow should have no other care save to be praying for those who give, and for the whole Church. And when she is asked a question by anyone, let her not straightway give an answer, except only concerning righteousness and faith in God; but let her send them that desire to be instructed to the rulers. And to those who question them let them the widows make answer only in refutation of idols and concerning the unity of God. But concerning punishment and reward, and the kingdom of the name of Christ, and His dispensation, neither a widow nor a layman ought to speak; for when they speak without the knowledge of doctrine, they will bring blasphemy upon the word. For our Lord likened the word of His tidings to mustard; but mustard, unless it be skilfully tempered, is bitter and sharp to those who use it. Wherefore our Lord said in the Gospel, to widows and to all the laity: *Cast not your pearls before swine, lest they trample upon them and turn against you and rend you* (Mt. 7:6). For when the Gentiles who are being instructed hear the word of God not fittingly spoken, as it ought to be, unto edification of eternal life — and all the more in that it is spoken to them by a woman — how that our Lord clothed Himself in a body, and concerning the passion of Christ: they will mock and scoff, instead of applauding the word of doctrine; and she shall incur a heavy judgement for sin.

It is neither right nor necessary therefore that women should be teachers, and especially concerning the name of Christ and the redemption of His passion. For you have not been appointed to this, O women, and especially widows, that you should teach, but that you should pray and entreat the Lord God. For He the Lord God, Jesus Christ our Teacher, sent us the Twelve to instruct the People and the Gentiles; and there were with us women disciples, Mary Magdalene and Mary the daughter of James and the other Mary; but He did not send them to instruct the people with us. For if it were required that women should teach, our Master Himself would have commanded these to give instruction with us. But let a widow know that she is the altar of God; and let her sit ever at home, and not stray or run about among the houses of the faithful to receive. For the altar of God never strays or runs about anywhere, but is fixed in one place.

A widow must not therefore stray or run about among the houses. For those who are gadabouts and without shame cannot be still even in their houses (cf. 1Tim. 5:13; Prov. 7:11); for they are no widows, but wallets, and they care for nothing else but to be making ready to receive. And because they are gossips and chatterers and murmurers, they stir up quarrels; and they are bold and shameless. Now they that are such are unworthy of Him who called them; for neither in the common assembly of rest of the Sunday, when they have come, are such women or men watchful, but they either fall asleep or prate about some other matter: so that through them others also are taken captive by the enemy Satan, who suffers not such persons to be watchful unto the Lord. And they who are such, coming in empty to the Church, go out more empty still, since they hearken not to that which is spoken or read to receive it with the ears of their hearts. Such persons, then, are like those of whom Isaiah said: *Hearing ye shall hear, and shall not understand; and seeing ye shall see, and shall not see. For the heart of this people is waxed gross, and with their ears they hear heavily, and their eyes they have shut: lest at any time they should see with their eyes, and hear with their ears* (Isa. 6:9–10). So in like manner the ears of such widows' hearts are stopped, because they will not sit beneath the roof of their houses and pray and entreat the Lord, but are impatient to be running after gain; and by their chattering they execute the desires of the Enemy. Now such a widow does not conform to the altar of Christ; for it is written in the Gospel: *If two shall agree together, and shall ask concerning any thing whatsoever, it shall be given them* (Mt. 18:19). *And if they shall say to a mountain that it be removed and fall into the sea, it shall so be done* (cf. Mt. 17:20; 21:21, etc).

Now we see that there are widows who esteem the matter as one of traffic, and receive greedily; and instead of doing good works and giving to the bishop for the entertainment of strangers and the refreshment of those in distress, they lend out on bitter usury; and they care only for Mammon, *whose god is* their purse and *their belly: for where their treasure is, there is also their heart* (Php. 3:19; Mt. 6:21). For she who is in the habit of roaming abroad and running about to receive takes no thought for good works, but serves Mammon and ministers to filthy lucre. And she cannot please God, nor is she obedient to His ministry, so as to be constantly praying and making intercession, because her mind is quite taken captive by the greed of avarice. And when she stands up to pray, she remembers whither she may go to receive somewhat; or else that she has forgotten to tell some matter to her friends. And when she stands in prayer, her mind is not upon her prayer, but upon that thought which has occurred to her mind. Now the prayer of such a one is not heard in regard to any thing. But she soon interrupts her prayer by reason of the distraction of her mind; for she does not offer prayer to God with all her heart, but goes off with the thought suggested by the Enemy, and talks with her friends about some unprofitable matter. For she knows not how she has believed, or of what order she has been accounted worthy.

But a widow who wishes to please God sits at home and meditates upon the Lord day and night, and without ceasing at all times offers intercession and prays with purity before the Lord (cf. 1 Tim. 5:5). And she receives whatever she asks, because her whole mind is set upon this. For her mind is not greedy to receive, nor has she much desire to make large expenses; nor does her eye wander, that she should see aught and desire it, and her mind be withdrawn; nor does she hear evil words to give heed to them, because she does not go forth and run about abroad. Therefore her prayer suffers no hindrance from any thing; and thus her quietness and tranquillity and modesty are acceptable before God, and whatsoever she asks of God, she presently receives her request. For such a widow, not loving money or filthy lucre, and not avaricious nor greedy, but constant in prayer, and meek and unperturbed, and modest and reverent, sits at home and works at her wool, that she may provide somewhat for those who are in distress, or that she may make a return to others, so that she receive nothing from them. For she bethinks her of that widow of whom our Lord gave testimony in the Gospel, who *came and cast into the treasury two mites, which is one dinar:* whom when our Lord and Teacher, the trier of hearts, saw, He said to us: O my disciples, *this poor widow hath cast in more alms than anyone; for everyone hath cast in of that which was super-*

fluous to him: but this, of all that she possessed she hath laid her up treasure (Mk. 12:41–44; cf. Mt. 6:20).

Widows ought then to be modest, and obedient to the bishops and the deacons, and to reverence and respect and fear the bishop as God. And let them not act after their own will, nor desire to do any thing apart from that which is commanded them, or without counsel to speak with any one by way of making answer, or to go to anyone to eat or drink, or to fast with anyone, or to receive aught of anyone, or to lay hand on and pray over anyone without the command of the bishop or the deacon. But if she do aught that is not commanded her, let her be rebuked for having acted without discipline. For whence knowest thou, O woman, from whom thou receivest, or from what ministry thou art nourished, or for whom thou fastest, or upon whom thou layest hand? For knowest thou not that concerning everyone of these thou shalt render an account to the Lord in the day of judgement, seeing that thou communicatest in their works? But thou, O widow who art without discipline, seest thy fellow widows or thy brethren in sickness, and hast no care to fast and pray over thy members, and to lay hand upon them and to visit them, but feignest thyself to be not in health, or not at leisure; but to others, who are in sins or are gone forth from the Church, because they give much, thou art ready and glad to go and to visit them. You then who are such ought to be ashamed; for you wish to be wiser and to know better, not only than the men, but even than the presbyters and the bishops. Know then, sisters, that whatsoever the pastors with the deacons command you, and you obey them, you obey God; and with whomsoever you communicate by the command of the bishop, you are without blame before God; and so is every brother of the laity who obeys the bishop and submits to him: for they (the bishops) are to render an account for all. But if you obey not the mind of the bishops and deacons, they indeed will be quit of your offences, but you shall render an account of all that you do of your own will, whether men or women.

Now whosoever prays or communicates with one that is expelled from the Church, must rightly be reckoned with him; for these things lead to the undoing and destruction of souls. For if one communicate and pray with him who is expelled from the Church, and obey not the bishop, he obeys not God; and he is defiled with him that is expelled. And moreover he suffers not that man to repent. For if no one communicate with him, he will feel compunction and weep, and will ask and beseech to be received again; and he will repent of what he has done, and will be saved.

That a woman should baptize, or that one should be baptized by a woman, we do not counsel, for it is a transgression of the commandment, and a great peril to her who baptizes and to him who is baptized. For if it were lawful to be baptized by a woman, our Lord and Teacher Himself would have been baptized by Mary His mother, whereas He was baptized by John, like others of the people. Do not therefore imperil yourselves, brethren and sisters, by acting beside the law of the Gospel.

But concerning envy or jealousy, or slander and fault-finding, or contention and ill-will, and carping or rivalry, we have already told you that these things ought not to be found in a Christian; but among widows it is not fitting that anyone of them should so much as be named. Yet because the author of evil has many wiles and devices, he enters into those who are no widows and boasts himself in them. For there are some indeed who profess themselves widows, but do not works worthy of their name. For not for the name of widowhood are they found worthy to enter into the kingdom, but for faith and works. For if one practise good works, she shall be praised and accepted; but if she practise evil works and do the works of the Evil One, she shall be blamed and cast out of the kingdom everlasting: because she has left the things eternal and desired and loved those that are temporal. Now we see and hear that there are widows in whom there is envy one towards another. For when thy fellow aged woman has been clothed, or has received somewhat from some one, thou oughtest, O widow, on seeing thy sister refreshed — if thou be a widow of God — to say: 'Blessed be God, who hath refreshed my fellow aged woman,' and to praise God; and afterwards to praise him that ministered, and say: 'May his work be acceptable in truth,' and: 'Remember him, Lord, for good in the day of Thy recompense, and my bishop who hath ministered well before Thee and hath dispensed the alms fairly; for my fellow aged woman was naked, and hath been provided: and add unto him glory, and give him also a crown of glory in the day of the manifestation of Thy coming.' And likewise also the widow who has received an alms of the Lord, let her pray for him that provided this ministration, suppressing his name like a wise woman, that his righteousness may be with God and not with men (cf. Mt. 6:1), — as He said in the Gospel: *When thou doest an alms, let not thy left hand know what thy rtght hand doeth* (Mt. 6:3) — lest, when thou pronounce and reveal his name in praying for him that gave, his name be disclosed and come to the ears of a heathen, and the heathen, being a man of the left hand, know it. Or it may even chance that one of the faithful, hearing thee, will go out and talk: and it is not expedient that those things which are done or spoken in the Church should come abroad and be revealed; for he that divulges and speaks of them disobeys God, and becomes a betrayer of the Church. But do thou in praying for him suppress his name; and so shalt thou fulfil that which is written, thou and the widows who are such as thou: for you are the holy altar of God, even of Jesus Christ.

But now we hear that there are widows who do not behave according to the commandment, but care only for this, that they may stray and run about asking questions. And moreover she who has received an alms of the Lord — being without sense, in that she discloses the matter to her that asks her — has revealed and declared the name of the giver; and the other, hearing it, murmurs and finds fault with the bishop who has dispensed, or with the deacon, or with him who has made some gift, saying: 'Knewest thou not that I was nearer to thee and in more distress than she?' And she knows not that it was not by man's will that this was done, but by the command of God. For if thou protest and say to him: 'I was nearer to thee, and thou knewest that I was more naked than she:' it behoved thee to know who it was that commanded, and to be silent and not find fault with him that ministered, but to go into thy house and fall upon thy face and give thanks to God for thy fellow widow; and to pray likewise for him that gave and for him that ministered, and to beseech the Lord that He would open to thee also the door of His favour. And the Lord would presently have heard thy prayer bountifully, and have sent thee more favour than thy fellow widow, from whence thou never thoughtest to receive a ministry; and such proof of thy patience would have been praiseworthy. Or know you not that it is written in the Gospel: *When thou doest an alms, sound not the trumpet before men to be seen of them, as the hypocrites do. For verily I say unto you, they have received their reward* (Mt. 6:2).

Now if God has commanded that a ministry be ministered in secret, and he that ministered did so minister: why then dost thou, who hast received in secret, proclaim it openly? Or thou, again who hast not received, why dost thou question it? For thou not only findest fault and murmurest, as one who is no widow, but even utterest a curse like the heathen. Or hast thou not heard what the Scripture saith: *Everyone that blesseth, is blessed; and everyone that curseth, is cursed* (cf. Num. 24:9; Gen. 27:29) And again in the Gospel He saith: *Bless them that curse you* (Lk. 6:28 (cf. Mt. 5:44)); and again: *When ye enter into a house, say: Peace be in this house. And if that house be worthy of peace, your peace shall come upon it; but if it be not worthy, your peace shall return unto you* (Mt. 10:12–13). If then peace returns to them that send it, much more will a curse return upon those who utter it idly: because that he upon whom it was sent does not merit to receive a curse. For everyone who curses a man idly, curses himself, since it is written in Proverbs: *As birds and fowl fly, so do idle curses return* (Prov. 26:2). And again He saith: *They that utter curses are void of understanding* (Prov. 10:18). For we are set forth in a parable by the example of the bee, as the Lord saith: *Go to the bee, and learn how she worketh. For her work she performeth in wisdom*;

and there is brought of her labour to be food for rich and poor. Beloved and praiseworthy is she, albeit she is little in strength (Prov. 6:8 LXX). As then the bee is *little in strength,* and when she has stung a man she loses her sting, and becomes barren and presently dies; so also we the faithful in like manner: whatever evil we do to another, we do it to ourselves; for, *Whatsoever thou hatest that it should be done to thee, thou shalt not do to another* (cf. Tob. 4:15; Did. 1:2). Wherefore, *everyone that blesseth is blessed* (cf. Num. 24:9).

Do you therefore admonish and rebuke those widows who are undisciplined and likewise exhort and encourage and help forward those who conduct themselves rightly. And let widows keep themselves from cursing, for they have been appointed to bless. Wherefore, let not the bishop, nor a presbyter, nor a deacon, nor a widow utter a curse out of their mouth, *that they may* not *inherit* a curse but *a blessing* (1 Pt. 3:9). And let this also be thy care, O bishop, that not even one of the laity utter from his mouth a curse: for thou hast the care of all.

Chapter XVI

On the appointment of Deacons and Deaconesses.

Wherefore, O bishop, appoint thee workers of righteousness as helpers who may co-operate with thee unto salvation. Those that please thee out of all the people thou shalt choose and appoint as deacons: a man for the performance of the most things that are required, but a woman for the ministry of women. For there are houses whither thou canst not send a deacon to the women, on account of the heathen, but mayest send a deaconess. Also, because in many other matters the office of a woman deacon is required. In the first place, when women go down into the water, those who go down into the water ought to be anointed by a deaconess with the oil of anointing; and where there is no woman at hand, and especially no deaconess, he who baptizes must of necessity anoint her who is being baptized. But where there is a woman, and especially a deaconess, it is not fitting that women should be seen by men: but with the imposition of hand do thou anoint the head only. As of old the priests and kings were anointed in Israel, do thou in like manner, with the imposition of hand, anoint the head of those who receive baptism, whether of men or of women; and afterwards — whether thou thyself baptize, or thou command the deacons or presbyters to baptize — let a woman deacon, as we have already said, anoint the women. But let a man pronounce over them the invocation of the divine Names in the water. And when she who is being baptized has come up from the water, let the deaconess receive her, and teach and instruct her how the seal of baptism ought to be kept unbroken in purity and holiness. For this cause we say that the ministry of a woman deacon is especially needful and important. For our Lord and Saviour also was ministered unto by women ministers, *Mary Magdalene, and Mary the daughter of James and mother of Jose, and the mother of the sons of Zebedee* (Mt. 27:56), with other women beside. And thou also hast need of the ministry of a deaconess for many things; for a deaconess is required to go into the houses of the heathen where there are believing women, and to visit those who are sick, and to minister to them in that of which they have need, and to bathe those who have begun to recover from sickness.

And let the deacons imitate the bishops in their conversation: nay, let them even be labouring more than he. And let them *not love filthy lucre* (1 Tim. 3:8); but let them be diligent in the ministry. And in proportion to the number of the congregation of the people of the Church, so let the deacons be, that they may be able to take knowledge of each severally and refresh all; so that for the aged women who are infirm, and for brethren and sisters who are in sickness — for every one they may provide the ministry which is proper for him.

But let a woman rather be devoted to the ministry of women, and a male deacon to the ministry of men. And let him be ready to obey and to submit himself to the command of the bishop. And let him labour and toil in every place whither he is sent to minister or to speak of some matter to anyone. For it behoves each one to know his office and to be diligent in executing it. And be you (bishop and deacon) of one counsel and of one purpose, and one soul dwelling in two bodies. And know what the ministry is, according as our Lord and Saviour said in the Gospel: *Whoso among you desireth to be chief, let him be your servant: even as the Son of Man came not to be ministered unto, but to minister, and to give his life a ransom for many* (Mt. 20:26–28). So ought you the deacons also to do, if it fall to you to lay down your life for your brethren in the ministry which is due to them. For neither did our Lord and Saviour Himself disdain ministering to us, as it is written in Isaiah: *To justify the righteous, who hath performed well a service for many* (Isa. 53:11). If then the Lord of heaven and earth *performed a service* for us, and bore and endured everything for us, how much more ought we to do the like for our brethren, that we may imitate Him. For we are imitators of Him, and hold the place of Christ. And again in the Gospel you find it written how our Lord *girded a linen cloth about his loins and cast water into a wash-basin,* while we reclined at supper, and drew nigh *and washed the feet of* us all *and wiped them with the cloth* (Jn. 13:4–5). Now this He did that He might show us charity and brotherly love, that we also should do in like manner one to another (cf. Jn. 13:14–15). If then our Lord did thus, will you, O deacons, hesitate to do the like for them that are sick and infirm, you who are workmen of the truth, and bear the likeness of Christ? Do you therefore minister with love, and neither murmur nor hesitate; otherwise you will have ministered as it were for men's sake and not for the sake of God, and you will receive your reward according to your ministry in the day of judgement. It is required of you deacons therefore that you visit all who are in need, and inform the bishop of those who are in distress; and you shall be his soul and his mind; and in all things you shall be taking trouble and be obedient to him.

Chapter XVII

On the upbringing of Orphan Children.

Now if anyone of the children of Christians be an orphan, whether boy or girl, it is well that, if there be one of the brethren who has no children, he should adopt the child in the place of children. And whoever has a son, let him adopt a girl; and when her time is come, let him give her to him to wife, that his work may be completed in the ministry of God. But if there be any who are unwilling to do thus because they would please men, and by reason of their riches are ashamed of orphan members: they who are such shall arrive at this very pass, and therein shall spend what they have spared; *and that which the saints have not eaten, the Assyrians shall eat and their land strangers shall devour before their eyes* (Isa. 1:7).

Do you therefore, O bishops, take pains over their upbringing, so that nothing may be wanting to them. And when a virgin's time is come, give her in marriage to one of the brethren. But when a boy is being brought up, let him learn a craft; and when he is become a man, let him receive the wage that is worthy of his craft, and let him fashion for himself the implements required for his craft, and not henceforth be a burden upon the love of the brethren, which was shown him without guile and without partiality.

And truly blessed is every one that is able to help himself, and shall not straiten the place of the orphan and the widow and the stranger. For woe from God to them that have, and receive in falsehood, or are able to help themselves and yet receive; for everyone of those who receive shall give an account to the Lord God in the day of judgement, how he received (cf. Did. 1:5; Herm. Mand. 2:5–6 (27:5–6)). If a man has received on account of a fatherless childhood, or on account of indigence in old age, or on account of infirmity and sickness, or on account of the rearing of children, he shall even be praised: for he is esteemed as the altar of God, therefore shall he be honoured of God. For he did not receive idly; because he was praying diligently and unremittingly at all times for those who give; for his prayer, which is his strength, he offered as his payment.

Those then who are such shall be declared blessed by God in the life everlasting.

But those who have, and receive under pretence, or else are slothful, and instead of working and helping others rather themselves receive, shall be held to account for that which they receive (cf. Did. 1:5; Herm. Mand. 2:5 (27:5)), because they have straitened the place of the faithful poor. For everyone who has some possession, and neither gives to others nor uses it himself, lays up for himself a perishable treasure on earth (Mt. 6:19); and he has inherited the place of the snake lying upon the treasure, and will come in danger of being reckoned with him. For whoever has, and receives in falsehood, puts his faith not in God but in the Mammon of iniquity (Lk. 16:9); and for the gain of avarice he holds the word in hypocrisy, and he is fulfilled in unbelief. Now such a one will come in danger of being reckoned with the unbelievers. But he who gives simply to every man, does well in giving, and he is innocent. He also who receives on account of distress, and uses sparingly those things which he has received, has received well; and he shall be praised by God in the life and rest everlasting (cf. Did. 1:5; Herm. Mand. 2:4–6 (27:4–6)).

CHAPTER XVIII

That it is not right to receive gifts of alms from reprehensible persons.

Do you the bishops and the deacons be constant therefore in the ministry of the altar of Christ, — we mean the widows and the orphans, — so that with all care and with all diligence you make it your endeavour to search out concerning the things that are given, and to learn of what manner is the conversation of him, or of her, who gives for the nourishment — we say again — of 'the altar.' For when widows are nourished from the fruits of righteous labour, they will offer a holy and acceptable ministry before Almighty God through His beloved Son and His holy Spirit: to whom be glory and honour for evermore.

Make it your care and endeavour therefore to minister to widows out of the ministry of a clean conscience, that what they ask and request may be granted them at once upon their praying for it. But if there be bishops who are careless and give no heed to these matters, through respect of persons, or for the sake of filthy lucre, or because they neglect to make inquiry; they shall render no ordinary account. For they receive, forsooth, to administer for the nourishment of orphans and widows, from rich persons who keep men shut up in prison, or ill-treat their slaves, or behave with cruelty in their cities, or oppress the poor; or from the lewd, and those who abuse their bodies; or from evildoers; or from forgers; or from dishonest advocates, or false accusers; or from hypocritical lawyers; or from painters of pictures; or from makers of idols; or from workers of gold and silver and bronze who are thieves; or from dishonest tax-gatherers; or from spectators of shows; or from those who alter weights or measure deceitfully; or from inn-keepers who mingle water with their wine; or from soldiers who act lawlessly; or from murderers; or from spies who procure condemnations; or from any Roman officials, who are defiled with wars and have shed innocent blood without trial: perverters of judgement who, in order to rob them, deal unjustly and deceitfully with the peasantry and with all the poor; and from idolaters; or from the unclean; or from those who practise usury, and extortioners. Now they who nourish widows from these sources shall be found guilty in judgement in the day of the Lord; for the Scripture has said: *Better is a supper of herbs with love and amity than the slaughter of fatted oxen with hatred* (Prov. 15:17). For if a widow be nourished with bread only from the labour of righteousness, it shall even be abundant for her; but if much be given her from the proceeds of iniquity it shall be insufficient for her. But again, if she be nourished from the proceeds of iniquity, she cannot offer her ministry and her intercession with purity before God; and even though she be righteous and pray for the wicked, her intercession for them will not be heard, but that for herself alone; for God makes trial of the hearts in judgement, and receives intercessions with discernment. But if they pray for those w ho have sinned and repent, their prayers will be heard. But those who are in sin, and do not repent, not only are they not heard when they pray, but they even call to remembrance their transgressions before the Lord.

Wherefore, a bishops, fly and avoid such ministrations; for it is written: *There shall not go up upon the altar of the Lord that which cometh of the price of a dog, or of the hire of a harlot* (Dt. 23:18). For if widows pray for fornicators and transgressors through your blindness, and be not heard, not receiving their requests, you will perforce bring blasphemy upon the word through your evil management, as though God were not good and ready to give.

Take good heed therefore that you minister not to the altar of God out of the ministrations of transgression. For you have no pretext to say, 'We do not know;' for you have heard that which the Scripture saith: *Depart from an evil man, and thou shalt not fear; and trembling shall not come nigh unto thee* (Isa. 54:14). But if you say: 'These are they alone who give alms; and if we receive not of them, from whence shall the orphans and widows and those in distress be provided?' God saith to you: 'To this end did you receive the gifts of the Levites, the first fruits and offerings of your people, that you might be sustained and even have over and above, that you might not be constrained to receive from evil persons.' But if the Churches are so poor that those in want must needs be supported by such, it were better for you rather to be wasted with famine than to receive from evil persons.

Search out and make trial, therefore, that you may be receiving from the faithful, who communicate with the Churches and conduct themselves well, wherewithal to nourish those in distress, and may not receive from those who are expelled from the Church until they are found worthy to be members of the Church. But if you are in want, tell the brethren, and let them treat together and give; and thus perform your ministrations in righteousness. And teach your people and tell them that it is written: *Honour the Lord with the fruits of righteous labour, and with the chiefest of all your increase* (Prov. 3:9). Wherefore, nourish and clothe those in want from the righteous labour of the faithful; and those things which are given by them, as we have already said, bestow for the ransom of the faithful; and redeem slaves and captives and prisoners, and those who are treated with violence, and those condemned by the mob, and those sentenced to fight with beasts, or to the mines, or to exile, and those condemned to the games. And let the deacons go in to those who are in distress, and let them visit each one and provide him with what he lacks.

But if ever it should happen that you are constrained and receive unwillingly some pieces of money from any evil person, you shall not employ them for the purchase of food; but if they be few, spend them on firewood for yourselves and for the widows, lest a widow, receiving of them, be forced to buy her some food with them. And so, unsullied by iniquity, the widows will pray and receive from God all good things for which they ask and make petition, all of them together and each one severally: and you also will not be reproached with these sins.

Chapter XIX

That it is a duty to take care of those who for the name of Christ suffer affliction as Martyrs.

You shall not turn away your eyes from a Christian who for the name of God and for His faith and love is condemned to the games, or to the beasts, or to the mines; but of your labour and of the sweat of your face do you send to him for nourishment, and for a payment to the soldiers that guard him, that he may have relief and that care may be taken of him, so that your blessed brother be not utterly afflicted. For let him that is condemned for the name of the Lord God be esteemed of by you as a holy martyr, an angel of God, or God upon earth, even one that is spiritually clothed with the Holy Spirit of God; for through him you see the Lord our Saviour, inasmuch as he has been found worthy of the incorruptible crown, and has renewed again the witness of His passion. To those therefore who are bearing witness it is the duty of all you the faithful to minister with care, and to refresh them out of your possessions through your bishop. But if there be a man who has nothing, let him fast, and that which would have been spent by him that day let him give for his brethren. But if thou art rich, thou must minister to them according to thy power, or even give thy whole possession and redeem them from bonds; for they it is who are worthy of God, and the sons who perform His will; as the Lord has said: *Every one that shall confess me before men, I also will confess him before my Father* (Mt. 10:32). And you shall not be ashamed to go to them where they are imprisoned. And when you do these things, you shall inherit everlasting life, for you become sharers of their martyrdom. For let us learn how our Lord said in the Gospel: *Come unto me, all ye blessed of my Father, inherit the kingdom which was prepared for you from before the foundations of the world. For I was hungry, and ye gave me to eat; and I was thirsty, and ye gave me to drink. I was a stranger, and ye gathered me; and I was naked, and ye covered me. I was sick, and ye visited me; and I was in prison, and ye came unto me. Then will the righteous answer and say: Our Lord, when saw we thee hungry, and gave thee to eat? or thirsty, and gave thee to drink? or naked, and covered thee? or sick, and did visit thee? or a stranger, and gathered thee? or in prison, and came unto thee? And he will answer and say to them:*

All that ye did to one of these little and mean ones, ye did it to me (Mt. 25:34–40). And then *shall they go into life everlasting* (Mt. 25:46).

But if there be one who is called a Christian, and he fall away and be tempted by Satan, and be convicted of evil deeds and condemned for his deeds, whether of theft or murder: avoid such persons, lest anyone of you be put on trial by those who seize him. For if one seize thee and question thee, and say to thee: 'Art thou also a Christian, like this man?' thou canst not deny that thou art a Christian, but must needs confess it. But thou wilt not be condemned as a Christian, but punished as a malefactor. For he asks thee whether thou art 'like this man:' and thy confession is rendered void. But if thou deny, thou hast also denied the Lord. Therefore avoid them, that you may be without offence. But the faithful who are violently and unjustly seized and imprisoned as evildoers, or even bound, help as your members with abundant care and with much pains, that you may deliver them from the hand of evil men. But if any man come near to them and be seized with them, and for no offence suffer affliction for his brother's sake, blessed is he in being called a Christian; for he has confessed the Lord, and he shall live before God. For if a man come near to those who are bound for the name of the Lord and be seized with them, he shall be blessed in being found worthy of such company.

And those again who are persecuted for the faith and pass from city to city (Mt. 10:23; 23:34), according to the Lord's command, do you receive and refresh; and when you receive them, rejoice, for you are made sharers of their persecution, For our Lord spoke concerning them in the Gospel thus: *Blessed are ye, when they shall persecute you and revile you for my name's sake* (Mt. 5:11). For when a Christian is persecuted and bears witness and is slain for the faith, he becomes a man of God (cf. 1 Tim. 6:11; 2 Tim. 3:17); and he is now no more persecuted by any man, for he has won him approval of the Lord. But if he deny, and say that he is not a Christian, he shall be called an offence; and though not persecuted by men, yet is he cast off by God for his denial; and he shall receive henceforth no portion with the saints in the kingdom everlasting, according to the Lord's promise, but his inheritance shall be with the ungodly. For the Lord God has said: *Whosoever shall deny me and my words before men, or shall be ashamed of me: I also will be ashamed of him, and will deny him before my Father who is in heaven* (Lk. 9:26;

Mt. 10:33), *when I come with power and glory to judge the dead and the living* (cf. Mt. 24:30; 2 Tim. 4:1). And again you find it written: *Every one that loveth his father or his mother more than me, is not worthy of me and everyone that loveth his son or his daughter more than me, is not worthy of me; and every one that taketh not up his cross rejoicing and glad and cometh after me, is not worthy of life; and every one that shall lose his life for my sake, shall find it; and every one that shall save his life, by denying, shall lose it. For what shall a man be profited if he acquire the whole world, and forfeit his soul? or what shall he give in exchange for his soul?* (Mt. 10:37–39; 16:25–26) And again: *Fear not them that kill the body, but are not able to kill the soul; but fear me rather, that am able to destroy soul and body in hell* (Mt. 10:28).

Now everyone who learns any craft watches his master and sees how by his skill and his knowledge he executes the work of his craft; and he himself copies him and executes the work which he has set him, that he may not be ill spoken of by him. But if he abate anything of the tasks set him, he is not perfect. We, then, who have our Lord for master and teacher, why do not we imitate His teaching and His conversation? For He left riches and favour, and power and glory, and came thus in poverty; and moreover He parted with Mary His blessed mother, and with His brethren, and with His life itself, and endured persecution even unto the cross. And these things He endured for our sake, that He might redeem us, who are of the People, from the bonds of the Second Legislation, of which we have already spoken, and might redeem you also, who are of the Gentiles, from the worship of idols and from all ungodliness, and get you for an inheritance. If then He suffered thus for our sake, to redeem us who believe in Him, and was not ashamed, why do not we also imitate His sufferings, while He gives us endurance? — and this for our own sake, that we may be delivered from the death of fire. For He endured for our sake, but we for our own sake. Or has our Lord any need that we should suffer for Him? Rather it is this alone that He desires, to make proof of the love of our faith, and of our free will. Let us then part with our parents and our kinsfolk, and with all that is in this world, and even with our life.

We must indeed pray that we *come not into temptation* (Mt. 26:41 (cf. 6:13)); yet if we be called to martyrdom, let us confess when we are interrogated, and when we suffer let us endure, and when we are afflicted let us rejoice, and when we are persecuted let us not grieve; for so doing, not only shall we deliver ourselves from hell, but we shall also teach those who are young in the faith, and the hearers, to do the like: and they shall live before God. But if we fail in faith towards the Lord, and deny through the infirmity of the body — as our Lord said: *The spirit is willing and ready, but the body is weak* (Mt. 26:41)— we shall not only destroy ourselves, but shall kill also our brethren with us. For when they see our denial, they will think that they have been made disciples of an erring doctrine; and when they stumble, we shall render an account for them as well as for ourselves, everyone of us, to the Lord in the day of judgement.

But if thou be taken and brought before the authority, and deny the hope that thou hast towards the Lord by thy holy faith, and thou be set at large to-day, but to-morrow fall sick of a fever and take to thy bed; or if thy stomach ail thee and retain no food, but vomit it out with grievous pains; or thou be afflicted with a disease of the belly, or with a disease in one of thy members; or thou bring up blood and bile from within thee by reason of dire disorders; or thou have an ulcer in one of thy members and be cut by the hands of physicians, and die in manifold afflictions and torments: what then will thy denial have availed thee which thou hast denied, O man? For behold, thy soul has inherited pains and afflictions, and thou hast destroyed thy life for ever before God; and thou shalt burn and be tormented without respite everlastingly: even as the Lord has said: *Everyone that loveth his life, shall lose it; and everyone that shall lose his life for my sake, shall find it* (Mt. 10:39). Now a Christian who denies, loves his life for a little while in this world, that he may not die for the name of the Lord God; but he has destroyed himself for ever in fire, for he has fallen of himself into Gehenna. For Christ has denied him, as He said in the Gospel: *Whosoever shall deny me before men, I also will deny him before my Father who is in heaven* (Mt. 10:33); but those whom the Lord has denied *they put forth and cast into the outer darkness: and there is their weeping and their gnashing of teeth* (Mt. 8:12; 22:13). For He said: *Everyone that loveth his life more than me, is not worthy of me* (Mt. 10:37; cf. Jn. 12:26).

Let us be earnest then to commit ourselves to the Lord God; and if any man be found worthy of martyrdom, let him accept of it with joy, seeing that he has been counted worthy of so great a crown, and that his departure from this world is by martyrdom. For the Lord our Saviour has said: *There is no disciple better than his master: but everyone shall be perfected as his master* (Lk. 6:40). Now our Lord consented to all these His sufferings that He might save us; and He submitted to be beaten, and that men should blaspheme Him and spit in His face, and to drink vinegar and gall; and at last He endured even to be hanged upon the cross. Let us therefore, who are His disciples, be also His imitators. For if He bore and endured all things for us, even to the sufferings of His passion, how much more ought we, for our own sakes, to be patient when we suffer? And we ought not to doubt; for so He has promised us, that if we should be burned with coals of fire, while we believe in our Lord Jesus Christ and in God His Father, the Lord God Almighty, and in His Holy Spirit, — to whom be glory and honour for evermore, Amen.

Chapter XX

Concerning the Resurrection of the Dead.

God Almighty will raise us up through God our Saviour, as He has promised. And He will raise us up from the dead even as we are — in this form in which we now are, but in the great glory of everlasting life, with nothing wanting to us. For though we be cast into the depths of the sea, or be scattered by the winds like chaff, we are still within the world; and the whole world itself is inclosed beneath the hand of God. From within His hand therefore will He raise us up: as the Lord our Saviour has said: *A hair of your head shall not perish; but in your patience ye shall possess your souls* (Lk. 21:18–19).

Now concerning the resurrection, and concerning the glory of the martyrs, the Lord spoke in Daniel thus: *Many that sleep in the breadth of the earth shall rise up in that day: some unto life everlasting, and some unto reproach and shame and dispersion. But they that understand shall shine as the luminaries which are in the heaven; and they that have been strengthened by the word, as the stars of heaven* (Dan. 12:2–3 LXX). As of the sun, then, and the moon, the luminaries of heaven, such glorious light has He promised to give to them *that understand* (Dan. 12:3), and confess His holy name, and bear witness.

But not to the martyrs alone has He promised the resurrection, but to all men; for He speaks thus in Ezekiel: [1]*The hand of the Lord came upon me: and the Lord brought me forth in the spirit, and set me in the midst of a valley: and it was full of bones.* [2]*And he caused me to pass over against them: and they were many, and they were exceeding dry.* [3]*And he said unto me: Son of man, shall these bones live? And I said: Thou knowest, Lord Adonai.* [4]*And the Lord said unto me: Prophesy unto these bones, and say to them: Ye dry bones, hear the word of the Lord.* [5]*Thus saith the Lord Adonai unto these bones: Behold, I will cause the spirit to enter into you, and ye shall live;* [6]*and I will put sinews upon you, and will build up flesh upon you, and will clothe you with skin; and I will give the spirit in you, and ye shall live: and ye shall know that I am the Lord.* [7]*And I prophesied as he spake unto me. And as I prophesied, there was made a sound and a movement;*

and the bones drew nigh, bone unto bone. [8]*And I saw that there came upon them sinews and flesh, and skin was stretched over them above: but there was no spirit in them.* [9]*And the Lord said unto me: Prophesy unto the spirit, and say: Thus saith the Lord Adonai: Come, spirit, from the four winds, and enter into these dead, and they shalt live.* [10]*And I prophesied, as he spake unto me: and the spirit entered into them, and they lived: and they stood upon their feet in a great army.* [11]*And the Lord said unto me: Son of man, these bones are the house of Israel; for they say: Our bones are dried up, and our hope is perished, and we are not.* [12]*Thus saith the Lord Adonai: Behold, I open your graves, and I will bring you forth from thence, O my people, and wilt bring you in to the land of Israel;* [13]*and ye shall know that I am the Lord, when I shall open your graves, to bring up my people from the graves.* [14]*And I will give my spirit in you, and ye shall live. And I will cause you to dwell in your land: and ye shall know that I am the Lord, that have spoken and have performed it* (Ezek. 37:1–14).

And all the inhabitants of the earth shall be silent, saith the Lord (Isa. 26:18). And again by Isaiah He said: *All they that sleep and are dead shall rise; and all they that are in the graves shall awake: for thy dew is a dew of healing unto them. But the land of the wicked shalt perish* (Isa. 26:19). And many other things also He said by Isaiah and by all the prophets concerning the resurrection and the life everlasting, and concerning the glory of the righteous; and as touching the wicked also, concerning their dishonour and exposure and downfall, and concerning their undoing and overthrow and condemnation. For that which He said, *the land of the wicked shall fall,* He speaks concerning their body; because it is of the earth, and shall be reckoned unto the earth in dishonour. Because they served not God, they shall fall into fire and torment. And in the Twelve Prophets again He speaks thus: *Behold, ye wicked, and see, and understand marvels: and return to corruption. For I do a work in your days, the which if a man recount it unto you, ye will not believe* (Hab. 1:5; Acts 13:41). Now these things, and many more than these, are spoken concerning those who believe not in the resurrection, and concerning those who deny God, and those who serve not God, and concerning transgressors of the law and the heathen; and when they shall see the glory of the faithful, they will be turned back to be destroyed in fire, because they believed not.

But we have learned and have believed; and by our Lord's resurrection from the dead is made sure to us the resurrection which God, who lies not, has promised us. For our Saviour, by rising Himself first, was made an earnest also of our resurrection. And those also who are called from the Gentiles, and even the heathen, read and hear concerning the resurrection that which is spoken and proclaimed to them by the Sibyl thus: *When all things have been made dust and ashes, God Most High will allay the fire, even he that kindled it. And then again will God himself raise up the bones and the ashes of men, and will clothe them with their form. For he will raise up men as they were before: and then shall be the judgement, wherein God will judge in the world to come. And the wicked and the ungodly the earth will cover again; but the just and the righteous shall live in the living world. And God will give them spirit and grace and life: and then shall they all see one another* (Orac. Sibyll. 4:179–185, 187, 189–190). And not only by the Sibyl, brethren, was the resurrection preached to the Gentiles, but by the holy Scriptures also our Lord proclaimed beforehand, to the Jews and the heathen and Christians at once, and announced the resurrection of the dead which is to be for men; and even by a dumb bird, we mean the Phoenix, which is but one alone, by means whereof God gives us again abundant demonstration of the resurrection. For if he had a mate, many would be seen by men; but now one only is seen, once in five hundred years. which enters Egypt and comes to the altar which is called 'of the Sun' bringing cinnamon. And as he prays toward the East, a fire is kindled of itself and burns him up, and he is reduced to ashes. And from the ashes again there is formed a worm; and it grows in his form and becomes a perfect Phoenix. And then he departs and goes away whence he came. If then by means of a dumb animal God shows us concerning the resurrection, we who believe in the resurrection and in the promise of God ought much more, as men deemed worthy of so great glory that we should receive an incorruptible crown in the life everlasting, to rejoice, if martyrdom come to us, in the great grace and in the honour and glory of martyrdom for God, and to accept of it joyfully with all our soul, and to believe in the Lord God who will raise us up in glorious light. As in the beginning God commanded by a word, and the world was made, and said: *Let there be light* (Gen. 1:3), and night and day, and heaven and earth and sea, and birds and living creatures of the sea, and creeping things of the earth and four-footed beasts, and trees; and everything was made by His word and established in its nature, as the

Scripture has said: these works themselves, which came into being through the obedience which they rendered Him, bear witness to God who made them that by Him they were made from that which was not; and they also show a sign of the resurrection. As then He made every thing, so will He the more rather quicken and raise up man, who is of His own forming. For if from that which was not He fashioned and established the world, much easier is this, that from that which is He should quicken and raise up man, who is the formation of His hands: even as also, in the human seed, He clothes man in the womb with a form and causes him to grow.

If then He raises up all men, — as He said by Isaiah: *All flesh shall see the salvation of God* (Isa. 40:5; 52:10), — much more will He quicken and raise up the faithful; and yet more again will He quicken and raise up the faithful of the faithful, who are the martyrs, and establish them in great glory and make them His counsellors. For to mere disciples, those who believe in Him, He has promised a glory as of the stars (Dan. 12:3); but to the martyrs He has promised to give an everlasting glory, as of the luminaries which fail not, with more abundant light, that they may be shining for all time.

As disciples of Christ, therefore, let us believe that we shall receive from Him all the good things which He has promised us in the life everlasting; and so let us imitate all His teaching and His patience. For as touching His birth from a virgin, and His coming, and the will of His passion, we have assurance through His holy Scriptures, even as the prophets foreannounced and foretold all things concerning His coming, and all have been accomplished and established in our hearts: for even the demons, trembling before His name (cf. Jas. 2:19), lauded His advent. Concerning those, therefore, which have come to pass of the things we have already mentioned, you also have believed and have been fully assured; but we yet more, who were with Him and have seen Him with our eyes, and have eaten with Him, and have been made the associates and witnesses of His coming (cf. Acts 10:41; 1 Jn. 1:1). As touching also His great and unspeakable gifts which He is yet to give us, according as He has promised, let us believe and hope that we shall receive them; for by this is all our faith put to the proof, if we believe in those His promises which are yet to be fulfilled. If then we are called to martyrdom for His name, and go forth from the world confessing Him, we shall be pardoned all sins and offences, and shall be found pure. For He spoke in David concerning the martyrs thus: *Blessed are they whose iniquity is forgiven, and whose sins are covered. Blessed is the man to whom the Lord shall not impute his sins* (Ps. 32:1–2a (31:1b–2a LXX)). Blessed therefore are the martyrs, and clear of all offences; for they have been removed and taken away from all iniquity: as He said in Isaiah of Christ and of His martyrs: *Behold, the righteous man is perished, and there is none that understandeth; and godly men are taken away, and no man layeth it to heart. For the righteous is gathered up from the presence of evil: and his burial shall be in peace* (Isa. 57:1–2a). Now these things are said of those who bear witness for the name of Christ.

But again, sins are *forgiven* by baptism also to those who from the Gentiles draw near and enter the holy Church of God. Let us inquire also, to whom sins are *not imputed.* To such as Abraham and Isaac and Jacob and all the patriarchs, as also to the martyrs. Let us hear then, brethren, for the Scripture saith: *Who shall boast himself and say: I am clear of sins? Or who shall be confident and say: I am innocent?* (Prov. 20:9) And again: *There is no man pure of defilement: not though his life be but one day* (Job 14:4–5 LXX). To everyone therefore who believes and is baptized his former sins have been *forgiven;* but after baptism also, provided that he has not sinned a deadly sin nor been an accomplice thereto, but has heard only, or seen, or spoken, and is thus guilty of sin. But if a man go forth from the world by martyrdom for the name of the Lord, *blessed* is he; for brethren who by martyrdom have gone forth from this world, of these *the sins are covered* (Ps. 32:1 (31:1 LXX)).

Chapter XXI

Concerning the Pascha and the Resurrection of Christ our Saviour.

Wherefore, a Christian ought to keep himself from vain speech and from words of levity and profanity. For not even on Sundays, in which we rejoice and make good cheer, is it permitted to anyone to speak a word of levity or one alien to religion: as our Lord also teaches us in the Psalm by David, saying thus: *And now, ye kings, understand; and be instructed, all ye judges of the earth, Serve the Lord with fear, and rejoice unto him with trembling. Give ye heed to discipline, lest the Lord be angry, and ye perish from the way of justice: for his wrath will shortly be kindled against you. Blessed are all they that trust on him* (Ps. 2:10–12). We must conduct our festivals and our rejoicings, then, with fear and trembling; for a faithful Christian, it saith, must not sing the songs of the heathen, nor have anything to do with the laws and doctrines of strange assemblies; for it may happen that through their songs he will make mention also of the name of idols, which God forbid that it should be done by the faithful; for the Lord by Jeremiah upbraids certain folk and speaks thus: *They have left me, and have sworn by them that be no gods* (Jer. 5:7). And again He saith: *If Israel will return, let him return unto me, saith the Lord; and if he will put away his abominations out of his mouth, and will fear before my face, and swear, As the Lord liveth* (Jer. 4:1–2). And again He saith: *I will take away the name of idols out of your mouth* (cf. Hos. 2:17; Zech. 13:2). And by Moses again He saith to them: *They have provoked me to jealousy by that which is no god; and with their idols they have angered me* (Dt. 32:21). And in all the Scriptures He speaks of these things.

And not by idols only is it not lawful for the faithful to swear, but neither by the sun, nor by the moon; for the Lord God speaks by Moses thus: *My people, if ye shall see the sun and the moon, ye shall not be led astray by them, and ye shall not serve them: for these have been given you for light upon the earth* (Dt. 4:19; Gen. 1:15). And by Jeremiah again He saith: *Ye shall not learn according to the ways of the gentiles; and ye shall not fear the signs of heaven* (Jer. 10:2). And by Ezekiel He speaks thus: *And he brought me in to the court of the house of the Lord, between the porch and the altar. And I saw there men whose backs were toward the temple of the Lord, and their faces toward the east: and they were worshipping the sun. And the Lord said unto me: Son of man, is this a light thing to the house of Judah to do these abominations which they do here, that they have filled the earth with iniquity, and have turned again to provoke me to anger? And they are become as scoffers: but I will deal with them in wrath; and mine eye shall not spare, and I will not have mercy. And they shall cry in mine ears with a loud voice, and I will not hear them* (Ezk. 8:16–18). You see, our beloved, how sternly and bitterly sentence is passed on those who worship the sun or swear thereby, that the Lord should *deal in His wrath* (Ezk. 8:18). Therefore it is not lawful for a believer to swear, neither by the sun nor by any other of the signs of heaven or the elements; nor to make mention with his mouth of the name of idols; nor to utter a curse out of his mouth, but rather blessings and psalms and words from the dominical and divine Scriptures, which are the firm foundation of our faith: and especially in the days of the Pascha, wherein all the faithful throughout the world fast; as our Lord and Teacher said when they asked Him: *Why do John's disciples fast, but thine fast not? And he answered and said to them: The sons of the bridechamber cannot fast, as long as the bridegroom is with them. But the days will come when the bridegroom shall be taken away from them: and then they shall fast in those days* (Mk 2.18–20 (Mt 9.14–15; Lk 5.33–35)). But now by His working is He with us, but visibly He is absent, because He has ascended to the heights of heaven and sat at the right hand of His Father.

Wherefore, when you fast, pray and intercede for them that are lost; as we also did when our Saviour suffered. For while He was yet with us before He suffered, as we were eating the Passover with Him, He said to us: *To-day, in this night, one of you will betray me. And we said unto Him, each one of us: Is it I, Lord? And he answered and said to us: He that putteth forth his hand with me into the dish* (Mk. 14:30; Mt. 26:21–23 (Mk. 14:18–20)). And Judas Iscariot, who was one of us, rose up and went his way to betray Him (cf. Jn. 13:30). Then our Lord said to us: *Verily I say unto you, a little while and ye will leave me; for it is written: I will strike the shepherd, and the lambs of his flock shall be scattered* (Jn. 16:32; Mt. 26:31; Mk. 14:27). And Judas came with the scribes and with the priests of the people, and betrayed our Lord Jesus.

Now this was done on the fourth day of the week. For when we had eaten the passover on the third day of the week at even, we went forth to the Mount of Olives; and in the night they seized our Lord Jesus. And the next day, which was the fourth of the week, He remained in ward in the house of Caiaphas the high priest. And on the same day the chiefs of the people were assembled and took counsel against Him. And on the next day again, which was the fifth of the week, they brought Him to Pilate the governor. And He remained again in ward with Pilate the night after the fifth day of the week. But when it drew on towards day on the Friday, *they accused him much* (Mk. 15:3) before Pilate; and they could show nothing that was true, but gave false witness against Him. And they asked Him of Pilate to be put to death; and they crucified Him on the same Friday.

He suffered, then, at the sixth hour on Friday. And these hours wherein our Lord was crucified were reckoned a day. And afterwards, again, there was darkness for three hours; and it was reckoned a night. And again, from the ninth hour until evening, three hours, reckoned a day. And afterwards again, there was the night of the Sabbath of the Passion. — But in the Gospel of

Matthew it is thus written: *At even on the sabbath, when the first day of the week drew on, came Mary Magdalene and the other Mary to see the tomb. And there was a great earthquake: for an angel of the Lord came down and rolled away the stone* (Mt. 28:1–2). — And again there was the day of the Sabbath; and then three hours of the night after the Sabbath, wherein our Lord slept. And that was fulfilled which He said: *The Son of man must pass three days and three nights in the heart of the earth* (Mt. 12:40), as it is written in the Gospel. And again it is written in David: *Behold, thou hast set my days in measure* (Ps. 38:6 LXX). Now because those days and nights came short, it was so written.

In the night, therefore, *when the first day of the week drew on,* He appeared to *Mary Magdalene and* to *Mary the daughter of James* (Mt. 28:1, 9 (cf. Jn. 20:1, 14; Mk. 16:1)); and in the morning of the first day of the week He went in to the house of Levi (cf. Gosp. of Peter 14); and then He appeared also to us ourselves. And He said to us, teaching us: Are ye fasting for Me these days? or have I any need that ye should afflict yourselves? But it is for your brethren that ye have done this; and do ye the same in these days when ye fast, and on the fourth of the week and on the Friday always, as it is written in Zechariah: *The fourth fast, and the fifth fast* (Zech. 8:19), which is the Friday. For it is not lawful to you to fast on the first of the week, because it is My resurrection; wherefore the first of the week is not counted in the number of the days of the Fast of the Passion, but they are counted from the second day of the week, and are five days. Wherefore, *The fourth fast, and the fifth fast, and the seventh fast, and the tenth fast shall be to the house of Israel* (Zech. 8:19). Fast then from the second day of the week, six days wholly, until the night after the Sabbath; and it shall be reckoned to you as a week. But *the tenth* (Zech. 8:19), — because the beginning of My name is Yod, — wherein was made the inception of the fasts. But fast not after the custom of the former People, but according to the new testament which I have appointed you: that you may be fasting for them on the fourth day of the week, because on the fourth of the week they began to destroy their souls, and apprehended Me. — For the night after the third of the week belongs to the fourth of the week, as it is written: *There was evening and there was morning, one day* (Gen. 1:5). The evening therefore belongs to the following day: for on the third of the week at even I ate My Pascha with you, and in the night they apprehended Me. — But fast for them also on the Friday, because thereon they crucified Me, in the midst of their festival of unleavened bread, as it is said of old in David: *In the midst of their festivals they set their signs, and they knew not* (Ps. 74:4 (73:4 LXX)).

"And be ye constant in fasting during these days always, and especially you who are of the Gentiles. For because the People was not obedient, I delivered them (the Gentiles) from blindness and from the error of idols and received them: that through your fast and theirs who are of the Gentiles, and your service during those days, when you pray and intercede for the error and destruction of the People, your prayer and intercession may be accepted before My Father who is in heaven, as though from one mouth of all the faithful on earth; and that all things which they did unto Me may be forgiven them. For this cause also I have already said to you in the Gospel: *Pray for your enemies* (cf. Mt. 5:44; Lk. 6:27), and: *Blessed are they that mourn* (Mt. 5:4), over the destruction of them that believe not."

Know therefore, our brethren, that as regards our fast which we fast in the Pascha, it is on account of the disobedience of our brethren that you are to fast. For even though they hate you, yet ought we to call them brethren; for we have it written in Isaiah thus: *Call them brethren that hate and reject you, that the name of the Lord may be glorified* (Isa. 66:5), For their sake therefore, and for the judgement and destruction of the holy place, we ought to fast and to mourn, that we may be glad and take our pleasure in the world to come; as it is written in Isaiah: *Rejoice, all ye that mourn over Zion* (cf. Isa. 66:10)*;* and again He saith: *To comfort all them that mourn over Zion: instead of ashes, the oil of gladness; and instead of a spirit afflicted with pain, a vesture of glory* (Isa. 61:2–3). We ought then to take pity on them, and to have faith and to fast and to pray for them. For when our Lord came to the People, they did not believe Him when He taught them, but put away His teaching from their ears. Therefore, because this People was not obedient, He received you, the brethren who are of the Gentiles, and opened your ears that your heart might hear; as our Lord and Saviour Himself said by the prophet Isaiah: *I appeared unto them that asked not after me, and I was found of them that sought me not; and I said, Behold, I am here, to a people that called not upon my name* (Isa. 65:1). Now of whom did He speak thus? Was it not of the Gentiles, because that they had never known God, and because that they were serving idols? But when our Lord came to the world and taught you, you believed, you who have believed in Him, that God is one (cf. Hermas Mand. 1:1); and they also who are worthy shall believe, until the number is filled up of them that are to be saved (cf. 1 Clem. 2:4; 59:2), *a thousand thousand, and ten thousand times ten thousand* (cf. Ps. 68:17 (67:18 LXX); Dan 7:10), as it is written in David.

But concerning the People, who believed not in Him, He said thus: *I spread forth my hands all the day long to a people that obey not and resist, and walk in a way that is not good, and go after their sins: a people that is provoking before me* (Isa. 65:2–3). See, then, that the People provoked our Lord in that they believed not in Him. Wherefore he saith: *They provoked the holy Spirit; and he was turned to enmity unto them* (Isa. 63:10). And again He speaks otherwise of them by Isaiah the prophet: *Land of Zebulun, land of Naphtali, the way of the sea, beyond Jordan, Galilee of the nations, a people that sitteth in darkness: ye have seen a great light; and they that sit in darkness and in the shadow of death, light is risen upon them* (Isa. 9:1–2; Mt. 4:15–16). *They that sit in darkness* He said concerning those who have believed in our Lord Jesus from among the People. For by reason of the blindness of the People a great darkness was round about them. For they saw Jesus, but that He is the Christ they knew not; and they understood Him not, neither from the writings of the prophets nor from His works and His healings. But to you of the People who have believed in Jesus we say: Learn how the Scripture bears witness to us and saith, *they have seen a great light.* You then who have believed in Him *have seen a great light,* even Jesus Christ our Lord; and they also shall see who are yet to believe in Him, But *they that sit in the shadow of death* are you who are of the Gentiles; for you were *in the shadow of death,* because you had set your hope on the worship of idols, and knew not God. But when Jesus Christ our Lord and Teacher appeared to us, *light rose upon you,* for you beheld and set your hope on the promise of the kingdom everlasting; and you have departed from the customs and practices of your former error, and no more serve idols as you were wont to serve them, but have already believed and been baptized in Him: and *a great light is risen upon you.*

Thus then, because the People were not obedient, they were made darkness; but the hearing of the ear of you who are of the Gentiles was made light (cf. Ps. 18:45 (17:45 LXX)). Wherefore, do you pray and intercede for them, and especially in the days of the Pascha, that by your prayers they may be found worthy of forgiveness, and may return to our Lord Jesus Christ.

It behoves you then, our brethren, in the days of the Pascha to make inquiry with diligence and to keep your fast with all care. And do you make a beginning when your brethren who are of the People keep the Passover. For when our Lord and Teacher ate the Passover with us, He was betrayed by Judas after that hour; and immediately we began to be sorrowful, because He was taken from us. By the number of the moon, as we count according to the reckoning of the believing Hebrews, on the tenth of the moon, on the second day of the week, *the priests and elders of the people assembled and came to the court of Caiaphas the high priest; and they took counsel to apprehend Jesus and put him to death: but they feared, saying: Not in the festival, lest the people make a tumult* (Mt. 26:3–5)*;* for all men *were hanging upon Him* (Lk. 19:48), and *they held him for a prophet* (Mt. 21:46) on account of His miracles of healing which He did among them. But *Jesus was* that day *in the house of Simon the leper* (Mt. 26:6), and we together with Him, and He related to us that which was about to happen to Him. But Judas went out privily from us, thinking that he would evade our Lord, and went to the house of

Caiaphas where the chief priests and elders were assembled, and said to them: *What will ye give me, and I will betray Him to you* when I have found an occasion? *But they appointed and gave him thirty pieces of silver* (Mt. 26:15). And he said to them: 'Make ready young men armed, because of His disciples, that if He go forth by night to a desert place I may come and lead you.' And they made ready the young men and prepared to seize Him. And Judas *was watching, when he might find him an occasion to betray him* (Mt. 26:16).

But by reason of the multitudes of all the people, from every city and from all the villages, who were coming up to the temple to keep the Passover in Jerusalem, the priests and elders took counsel and commanded and appointed that they should keep the festival straightway, that they might seize Him without disturbance. For the inhabitants of Jerusalem were engaged with the sacrifice and the eating of the Passover; and moreover, all the people that were without were not yet come, for they had deceived them as to the days. That they might be convicted before God of erring utterly in all things, therefore they anticipated the Passover by three days, and kept it on the eleventh of the moon, on the third day of the week. For they said: 'Because the whole people is gone astray after Him, now that we have an occasion let us seize Him; and then, when all the people are come, let us put Him to death before all, that this may be known openly, and all the people may turn back from after Him.'

And so in the night when the fourth day of the week drew on, Judas betrayed our Lord to them. But they made the payment to Judas on the tenth of the month, on the second day of the week; wherefore they were accounted by God as though on the second day of the week they had seized Him, because on the second of the week they had taken counsel to seize Him and put Him to death; and they accomplished their malice on the Friday: as Moses had said concerning the Passover, thus: *It shall be kept by you from the tenth until the fourteenth: and then all Israel shall sacrifice the passover* (Ex. 12:6).

Therefore you shall fast in the days of the Pascha from the tenth, which is the second day of the week; and you shall sustain yourselves with bread and salt and water only, at the ninth hour, until the fifth day of the week. But on the Friday and on the Sabbath fast wholly, and taste nothing. You shall come together and watch and keep vigil all the night with prayers and intercessions, and with reading of the Prophets, and with the Gospel and with Psalms, with fear and trembling and with earnest supplication, until the third hour in the night after the Sabbath; and then break your fasts. For thus did we also fast, when our Lord suffered, for a testimony of the three days; and we were keeping vigil and praying and interceding for the destruction of the People, because that they erred and confessed not our Saviour. So do you also pray that the Lord may not remember their guilt against them unto the end for the guile which they used against our Lord, but may grant them a place of repentance and conversion, and forgiveness of their wickedness.

For he who was a heathen and of a foreign people (cf. Gosp. of Peter 1), Pilate the judge, did not consent to their deeds of wickedness, but *took water and washed his hands, and said: I am innocent of the blood of this man* (Mt. 27:24). But the People answered and said: *His blood be upon us, and upon our children* (Mt. 27:25); and Herod commanded that He should be crucified (cf. Gosp. of Peter 1); and our Lord suffered for us on the Friday. Especially incumbent on you therefore is the fast of the Friday and of the Sabbath; and likewise the vigil and watching of the Sabbath, and the reading of the Scriptures, and psalms, and prayer and intercession for them that have sinned, and the expectation and hope of the resurrection of our Lord Jesus, until the third hour in the night after the Sabbath. And then offer your oblations; and thereafter eat and make good cheer, and rejoice and be glad, because that the earnest of our resurrection, Christ, is risen. And this shall be a law to you for ever, unto the end of the world. For to those who have not believed in our Saviour He is dead, because their hope in Him is dead; but to you who believe, our Lord and Saviour is risen, because your hope in Him is immortal and living for ever.

Fast then on the Friday, because thereon the People killed themselves in crucifying our Saviour; and on the Sabbath also, because it is the sleep of our Lord; for it is a day which ought especially to be kept with fasting: even as blessed Moses also, the prophet of all things touching this matter, commanded. For because he knew by the Holy Spirit and it was commanded him by Almighty God, who knew what the People were to do to His Son and His beloved Jesus Christ, — as even then they denied Him in the person of Moses, and said: *Who hath appointed thee head and judge over us?* (Ex.

2:14) — therefore he bound them beforehand with mourning perpetually, in that he set apart and appointed the Sabbath for them. For they deserved to mourn, because they denied their Life, and laid hands upon their Saviour and delivered Him to death. Wherefore, already from that time there was laid upon them a mourning for their destruction.

But let us observe and see, brethren, that most men in their mourning imitate the Sabbath; and they likewise who keep Sabbath imitate mourning. For he that mourns kindles no light: neither do the People on the Sabbath, because of the commandment of Moses; for so it was commanded them by him (cf. Ex. 35:3). He that mourns takes no bath: nor yet the People on the Sabbath. He that mourns does not prepare a table: neither do the People on the Sabbath, but prepare and lay for themselves the evening before (cf. Ex. 16:29); because they have a presentiment of mourning, seeing that they were to lay hands on Jesus. He that mourns does no work, and does not speak, but sits in sorrow: so too the People on the Sabbath; for it was said to the People concerning the mourning of the Sabbath thus: *Thou shalt not lift thy foot to do any work, and thou shalt speak no word out of thy mouth* (Isa. 58:13 LXX). Now who testifies that the Sabbath is a mourning for them? The Scripture testifies, and saith: *Then shall the people lament, family over against family: the family of the house of Levi apart, and their women apart; the house of Judah apart, and their women apart* (Zech. 12:12–13)*:* even as, after the mourning of Christ until now, on the ninth of the month of Ab (August) they come together and read the Lamentations of Jeremiah and wail and lament. Now nine represents *Theta;* but *Theta* denotes God. For God therefore they lament, even for Christ who suffered — rather, on account of God our Saviour, but over themselves and their own destruction. Does any man lament, brethren, except he have a grief? Therefore do you also mourn for them on the day of the Sabbath of the Pascha until the third hour in the night following; and thereafter, in the Resurrection of Christ, rejoice and make good cheer for their sake, and break your fast; and the surplus of your fast of six days offer to the Lord God, And let those of you who have abundance or worldly possessions minister diligently to those who are poor and needy and refresh them, that the reward of your fast may be received.

Wherever, then, the Fourteenth of the Pascha falls, so keep it; for neither the month nor the day squares with the same season every year, but is variable. When therefore that People keeps the Passover, do you fast; and be careful to perform your vigil within their feast of unleavened bread. But on the first day of the week make good cheer at all times; for he is guilty of sin, whosoever afflicts his soul on the first of the ac week. And hence it is not lawful, apart from the Pascha, for anyone to fast during those three hours of the night between the Sabbath and the first of the week, because that night belongs to the first of the week; but in the Pascha alone you are to fast these three hours of that night, being assembled together, you who are Christians, in the Lord.

Chapter XXII

That Children should be taught Crafts.

And teach your children crafts that are agreeable and befitting to religion, lest through idleness they give themselves to wantonness. For if they are not corrected by their parents, they will do those things that are evil, like the heathen. Therefore spare not to rebuke and correct and teach them (cf. Prov. 23:13); for you will not kill them by chastising them, but rather save them alive: as our Lord also teaches us in Wisdom, saying thus: *Chasten thy son, that there may be hope for him* (Prov. 19:18)*: for thou shalt strike him with a rod, and deliver his soul from Sheol* (Prov. 23:14). And He saith again: *Whosoever spareth his rod, hateth his son* (Prov. 13:24). Now our rod is the Word of God, Jesus Christ: even as Jeremiah also saw Him as *an almond rod* (Jer. 1:11–12). Every man accordingly who spares to speak a word of rebuke to his son, hates his son. Therefore teach your sons the word of the Lord, and punish them with stripes, and bring them into subjection from their youth by your word of religion. And give them no liberty to set themselves up against you their parents; and let them do nothing without your counsel, lest they go with those of their own age and meet together and carouse; for in this way they learn mischief, and are caught and fall into fornication. Now, whether this happen to them without their parents, their parents themselves will be accountable before God for the judgement of their souls; or whether again by your licence they are undisciplined and sin, you their parents will likewise be guilty on their account before God. Therefore be careful to take wives for them, and have them married when their time is come, lest in their early age by the ardour of youth they commit fornication like the heathen, and you have to render an account to the Lord God in the day of judgement.

Chapter XXIII

On Heresies and Schisms.

Before all things beware of all abominable and evil and bitter heresies, and fly from them as from a blazing fire, and from those who adhere to them. For if when a man makes a schism, he condemns himself to fire together with those who go astray after him, how much more if one go and sink himself in the heresies. For know this, that if any of you covet the primacy and dare to make a schism, he shall inherit the place of Korah and Dathan and Abiram, he and they that are with him, and with them he shall be condemned to fire (Num. 16:1–33). For even the adherents of Korah were Levites, and ministered in the tabernacle of witness; but they coveted the primacy, and desired the high priesthood; and they began to speak evil of the great Moses, because, said they, he is married to a heathen woman — *for he had an Ethiopian wife* (Num. 12:1)— and is defiled with her; and many others, and they of the following of Zimri, who committed fornication with the Midianite women (Num. 25:1–8), are with him. And the people, said they, that are with him are defiled; and his brother Aaron, too, was the author of idolatry, who made for his people the molten and graven image. And they spoke evil of Moses, who wrought so many mighty works and signs from God for the People; who did these excellent and marvellous works for their benefit; who brought the ten plagues upon the Egyptians; who divided the Red Sea that the waters stood up as a wall on this side and on that, and caused the People to pass over as in the dry desert, and drowned their enemies and them that evil entreated them, and all that were with them; who made sweet for them the fountain of water, and brought them forth streams from the flinty rock, so that they drank and were satisfied; who brought them down manna from heaven, and with the manna gave them also flesh; who gave them a pillar of fire by night for light and guidance, and a cloud by day for a covert, and in the desert stretched forth the hand to them for the dispensation of the Law, and gave them the Ten Words of God. And they spoke evil against the friend and good servant of the Lord God, as men glorying in righteousness, and boasting of holiness, and making a show of purity, and in hypocrisy making a display of service.

And thus, as puritans and sticklers for holiness, they said: 'Let us not be polluted with Moses and the people that is with him, because they are defiled.' And there rose up two hundred and fifty men, and they (Korah, etc.) led them astray to forsake the great Moses, that men might suppose concerning them that they were giving God more glory and ministering to Him more zealously. For among that multitude of the people aforesaid but one censer of incense was offered to the Lord God; but they who were in the schism, two hundred and fifty men with their leaders, offered each one a censer of incense, two hundred and fifty censers, as though forsooth they were far more religious and pure and zealous than Moses and Aaron and the people that was with them. But the more numerous ministry of those in the schism availed them nothing, but *fire was kindled from before the Lord, and devoured them; and those two hundred and fifty men were burned up, holding the censers in their hands* (Num. 16:35). *And the earth opened her mouth and swallowed up Korah and Dathan and Abiram, and their tents and their vessels, and all that were with them: and they went down alive to Sheol* (Num. 16:32–33) unto punishment. And thus were the error-leaders of the schism swallowed up by the earth; and those two hundred and fifty men who went astray were burned with fire while the whole people beheld it. But the most of the people the Lord spared, among whom were many sinners, whom the Lord would judge each according to his works. And the most of the people He spared; but those who supposed that they were pure and holy, and performing a better ministry, the fire devoured, because that they were in the schism. *And the Lord said to Moses and to Aaron: Take the censers of brass from the midst of the burning, and make of them fine plates, and overlay the altar therewith; that the children of Israel may see, and no more do so. And scatter the strange fire there; because it hath sanctified the censers of them that were sinners in their souls* (Num. 16:36–38).

Let us regard therefore and see, beloved, the end of the schismatics, what befell them. For though they should appear pure and holy and chaste, their last end is given unto fire and burning everlasting. Let this then inspire you with fear, that even the fire of the schismatics was judged with fire: not because it *sanctified the censers,* but because they *in their souls* sanctified them; that is, forasmuch as the fire was performing its work, they also supposed in their heart, and *in their souls,* that their censers were holy. For it behoved the fire, which was employed for the ministry of transgression and the provocation of God, not to obey them but to cease from its operation, or to be quenched, and not to devour or burn or consume that which was put upon it. But now, because it did not the will of the Lord God, but obeyed the schismatics, therefore it was said: *And scatter also the strange fire there;* that is, with fire the Lord judgeth the fire (cf. Isa. 66:16).

If therefore upon those schismatics, who supposed that they were glorifying God, this threat and judgement was laid, what will happen to these heretics who blaspheme Him? Do you then, when you see from the Scriptures with the eyes of faith the plates of brass laid over the altar, beware of making schisms. For the adherents of Korah, Dathan and Abiram were made a monument and example of the destruction of schismatics; and everyone who imitates them shall perish even as they. As men therefore who believe and know, keep yourselves far from schisms, and go not near them in any wise: as Moses said concerning them to the people: *Separate yourselves from among these stubborn men, and come not near to any thing that is theirs, lest ye perish with them in all their sins* (Num. 16:26). And when the anger of the Lord had burned against the schismatics, it is written that the people fled from them, and said: *Lest the earth swallow us* (Num. 16:34) also with them. So then do you also, as men contending for their lives, flee from schisms; and those who would do any such thing reject, for you know the place of their condemnation.

But as for heresies, be unwilling even to hear their names, and defile not your ears with them; for not only do they in no wise glorify God, but they verily blaspheme against Him. Wherefore, the heathen are judged because they have not known, but the heretics are condemned because they withstand God: as also our Lord and Saviour Jesus said: *There shall be heresies and schisms* (cf. 1 Cor. 11:19): and again: *Woe unto the world because of scandals. For it must needs be that scandals and schisms come: yet woe to the man by whom they come* (Mt. 18:7).

Then indeed we did but hear, but now we have also seen, even as the Scripture declares by Jeremiah saying: *Defilement is gone forth in all the earth* (Jer. 23:15). Now these *defilements,* of heresies, *are gone forth;* and they have come about for the persuasion of our hearts, and for the confirming of our belief that those things which were foretold are true; for behold, they have come to pass and are accomplished. For all the working of the Lord our God has passed from the People to the Church through us the Apostles; and He has withdrawn Himself and left the People, as it is written in Isaiah: *He hath left his people the house of Jacob* (Isa. 2:6); and: *Jerusalem is deserted, and Judah is fallen. And their tongues are busy with iniquity, and they obey not the Lord* (Isa. 3:8); and: *I will leave my vineyard* (cf. Isa. 5:6); and: *Behold, your house is left to you desolate* (Mt. 23:38).

He has left that People, therefore, and has filled the Church; and He has accounted her a mountain of habitation, and throne of glory, and lofty house, as He said in David: *The mount of the Lord is a mountain of fatness, a mountain of peaks. What think ye of the mountain of peaks? It is the mountain which the Lord hath chosen him to dwell therein: the Lord shall abide therein for ever* (Ps. 67:16–17 LXX). You see then how He saith to others: *What think ye*? even to those who err in thinking that there are other churches: for one is she that is the mountain of God's sanctuary. And by Isaiah He said again: *In the last days the mountain of the house of the Lord, the God of Jacob, shall be established on the top of the mountains, and higher than the hills; and all nations shall look unto it; and many peoples shall go and say: Come, let us go up to the mountain of the Lord, and to the house of the God of Jacob; and he shall teach us his way, and we will go therein* (Isa. 2:2–3). And again He said: *There shall be signs and wonders in the midst of the people from the Lord of Sabaoth, and him that dwelleth in Mount Zion* (Isa. 8:18). And again by Jeremiah He said: *A high throne is our sanctuary* (Jer. 17:12). As then He left the People, so did He leave their temple to them desolate; and He rent the veil, and took away from it the Holy Spirit, and shed Him upon them that believed from among the Gentiles, as He said by Joel: *I will pour out of my spirit upon all flesh* (Joel 2:28). For He took away the Holy Spirit, and the power of the word, and all the ministry from that People, and set it in His Church. Now in like manner did Satan also, the tempter, depart from that People and come against the Church. And he now no longer tempts that People, because by their evil works they have fallen into his hands, but he has set about to tempt the Church and to exercise his agency in her. And he has raised up against her afflictions and persecutions, and blasphemies and heresies and schisms. Formerly indeed, in that time, there were heresies and schisms in that People; but now Satan by his evil agency has driven forth some that were of the Church, and has made heresies and schisms.

Now the beginning of heresies was on this wise. Satan clothed himself in a certain Simon, one that was a magician and his minister of old; and when we, by the gift of the Lord our God and by the power of the Holy Spirit, were working miracles of healing in Jerusalem, *and by the laying on of our hand the fellowship of the Holy Spirit was given* (cf. Acts 8:17–19) to those who drew nigh to the faith, then *he offered* us much *money* (Acts 8:18), and desired that, as he had deprived Adam of the knowledge of life through eating of the tree, so by the gift of money he might deprive us also of the gift of God, and might take captive our minds with the bestowal of possessions, to the end that we should barter away and give to him for money the power of the Holy Spirit. Hereupon were we all stirred up; then Peter looked upon Satan, who was dwelling in Simon, and said to him: *Thy money go with thee to perdition: but thou shalt have no part in this word* (Acts 8:20–21).

But when we had divided the whole world into twelve parts, and were gone forth among the Gentiles into all the world to preach the word (cf. Mk. 16:15; Mt. 28:19), then Satan set about and stirred up the People to send after us false apostles for the undoing of the word. And he sent out from the People one whose name was Cleobius, and joined him to Simon, and others also after them. Now the party of Simon followed hard upon me Peter, and came to corrupt the word. And when he was in Rome he disturbed the Church much and subverted many; and he even made a show as though he would fly. And he was capturing the Gentiles, moving them by the power and agency of his magic arts. And on a certain day I went and saw him flying in the air; then I stood still, and said: 'By the power of the name of Jesus I cut off thy powers.' And he fell and broke the ankle-bone of his foot. And then many turned back from him; but others, worthy of him, continued with him. And thus was that his heresy first established. And by other false prophets beside was the enemy working. And they all had one law upon earth, that they should not employ the Torah and the Prophets, and that they should blaspheme God Almighty, and should not believe in the resurrection. And in other respects they were teaching and disturbing men with many opinions. For many of them taught that a man should not marry, saying that if one did not marry, this was holiness; and in the name of holiness they were commending the tenets of their heresies. Others again of them taught that a man might not eat flesh, saying that no one might eat any thing wherein there is a soul. But others said that one was bound to abstain from swine's flesh only, but might eat those things which the Law pronounces clean, and that he should be circumcised according to the Law. And some taught this, and some that, causing contentions and disturbing the Churches.

Chapter XXIV

On the ordering of the Church: showing also that the Apostles came together for the correction of abuses.

Now already we had rightly preached the holy word of the Catholic Church; and we returned once more to come to the Churches, and found men occupied with other opinions. For some forsooth were observing holiness; and some abstained from flesh and from wine, and some from swine's flesh; and they were observing some or other of all the bonds which are in the Second Legislation.

When therefore the whole Church was in peril of falling into heresy, all we the twelve Apostles came together to Jerusalem and took thought what should be done. And *it seemed good to us, being all of one accord* (Acts 15:25), to write this Catholic Didascalia for the confirming of you all. And we have established and set down therein that you worship God Almighty and Jesus Christ and the Holy Spirit; that you employ the holy Scriptures, and believe in the resurrection of the dead; and that you make use of all His creatures with thanksgiving (cf. 1Tim. 4:3); and that men should marry: for He saith in Proverbs: *Of God is a woman betrothed to a man* (Prov. 19:14); and in the Gospel again our Lord saith: *He that created from the beginning the male, said that he created also the female. Therefore a man shall leave his father and his mother, and shall cleave to his wife: and they two shall be one body. What therefore God hath coupled, let not man separate* (Mt. 19:4–6; Gen. 2:24). But sufficient for the faithful is the circumcision of the heart, which is spiritual, as He said by Jeremiah: *Light you a lamp, and sow not among thorns. Be circumcised unto the Lord your God, and circumcise the foreskin of your heart, ye men of Judah* (Jer. 4:3–4). And again in Joel He saith: *Rend your hearts, and not your garments* (Joel 2:13). And as for baptism also, one is enough for you, even that which has perfectly forgiven you your sins. For Isaiah said not only *Wash,* but *Wash, and be cleansed* (Isa. 1:16).

Now we had much questioning, as men contending for life; and not we the Apostles only, but also the people, together with James the bishop of Jerusalem, who is our Lord's brother after the flesh, and with his presbyters and deacons and all the Church. For also some days before, *certain men had come down from Judaea to Antioch, and were teaching the brethren, saying: Except ye be circumcised and conduct yourselves according to the law of Moses,* and keep yourselves clean from meats, and all the rest, *ye cannot be saved; and they had much conflict and questioning* (Acts 15:1–2), And when the brethren of Antioch knew that we were all assembled and come to make inquiry of these matters, they sent to us certain men that were believers and had knowledge. of the Scriptures to learn concerning this question, *And when they were come to Jerusalem, they related to us* (Acts 15:4) the controversy which they had in the Church of Antioch, *And there rose up certain men who had believed from the sect of the Pharisees, saying: Ye ought to be circumcised and to keep the law of Moses* (Acts 15:5). And others also were crying out and saying in like manner. Then I *Peter rose up and said to them: 'Men, brethren, ye yourselves know that from the first days when I was among you, God made choice that by my hands the gentiles should hear the gospel and believe. And God, who proveth the hearts, gave witness of them* (Acts 15:7–8); for to Cornelius, a certain centurion, there had appeared an angel and told him of me; and he sent for me. But when I was ready to go to him, it was shown me concerning the Gentiles that they were about to believe, and concerning all meats. For I [9]*had gone up to a housetop to pray;* [11]*and I saw the heavens opened, and a certain vessel, that was tied by its four corners, being lowered and let down upon the earth;* [12]*and there were therein all manner of four-footed beasts and creeping things of the earth and fowls of the heaven.* [13]*And there came to me a voice saying: Simon, arise, slay and eat.* [14]*But I said: God forbid, Lord, for I have never eaten any thing defiled and profane.* [15]*And there came to me again another voice, the second time, saying: W hat God hath made clean, do not thou make profane.* [16]*Now this was done thrice: and the vessel was taken up to heaven* (Acts 10:9–16 (11:4–10)). Thereupon *I bethought me, and understood the word of the Lord* (Acts 11:16), *how that He had said: Rejoice, ye gentiles, with the people* (Dt. 32:43 (Rom 15:10)), and that everywhere He had spoken of the calling of the Gentiles; and I rose up and went my way. And when I was entered into his house and had begun to speak the word of the Lord, the Holy Spirit lighted down upon him and upon all the Gentiles that were there present (Acts 11:15). God, then, *hath given the Holy Spirit to them even as to us, and hath made no distinction between us and them in the faith, and he hath cleansed their hearts. Now therefore, why tempt ye God, that ye should lay a yoke upon the necks of the disciples which nei-*

ther our fathers nor we were able to bear? But by the grace of our Lord Jesus Christ we believe that we shall be saved even as they also (Acts 15:8–11). For our Lord came and released us from those bonds, and said: *Come unto me, all ye that toil and are laden with heavy burdens, and I will give you rest. Take my yoke upon you, and learn of me; for I am gentle and lowly in heart: and ye shall find rest unto your souls. For my yoke is pleasant, and my burden is light* (Mt. 11:28–30). If then our Lord has released and unburdened us, why will ye lay snares for your own selves?'

[13]*Then all the people was silent; and I James answered and said: Men, brethren, hear me.* [14]*Simon hath told how formerly God said that he would choose him out a people from the gentiles to his name:* [15]*whereunto agree the words of the prophets, as it is written:* [16]*Hereafter will I raise up and build the tabernacle of David, that is fallen; and the ruins thereof will I build and raise up;* [17]*that the residue of men may seek the Lord, and all the gentiles upon whom my name is called,* [18]*saith the Lord who maketh known these things from everlasting.* [19]*Wherefore I say, that no man vex them that turn to God from among the gentiles,* [20]*but that word be sent them on this wise: that they abstain from evil practices, and from idols, and from that*

which is sacrificed, and from that which is strangled, and from blood. [22]*Then* we *the apostles* and the bishops *and the elders, together with the whole church, thought it well to choose out men front amongst them and send them to Antioch in company with Barnabas and Paul,* who were come thence. And we chose and appointed *Judas, who was called Barsabbas, and Silas, notable men among the brethren,* [23]*and wrote by them as followeth: —The apostles and elders and brethren to the brethren who are of the gentiles in Antioch and Syria and Cilicia, greeting.* [24]*Forasmuch as we have heard that some have troubled you with words, that they might corrupt your souls, whom we sent not:* [25]*we have determined, being all assembled together, to choose out and send men unto you with our beloved Barnabas and his companions,* whom ye sent hither. [27]*And we have sent Judas and Silas, who themselves will tell you of these things by word of mouth. For it hath seemed good to the Holy Spirit, and to us, that no further burden be laid upon you, save that ye abstain from these necessary things:* [29]*from that which is sacrificed, and from blood, and from that which is strangled, and from fornication. And from these keep yourselves, and do well. Fare ye well* (Acts 15:13–29).

Now the epistle we sent; but we ourselves remained in Jerusalem many days; and we were consulting and ordering together those things which were for the advantage of all the people, and writing also this Catholic Didascalia.

Chapter XXV

Showing that the Apostles returned once more to the Churches and set them in order.

Now the decision which we reached with counsel and thought concerning those who have already gone astray, we have thus affirmed and established. And we will return yet again and go to the Churches a second time, as in the beginning of the preaching, and will confirm the faithful that they may avoid the offences aforesaid, and may not receive those who come deceitfully in the name of apostles, but may know them by the changeableness of their words and by the performance of their works. For these are they of whom our Lord said: *There shall come unto you men having on the clothing of lambs, but inwardly ravening wolves: and by their fruits ye shall know them* (Mt. 7:15–16a). *Beware of them therefore. Now there shall arise false Christs and lying prophets, and lead many astray; and by reason of manifold iniquity the love of many shall wax cold. But he that shall endure unto the end, the same shall be saved* (Mt. 24:11–13, 24).

Now let those who have not erred, and those also who repent of their error, be left in the Church. But as for those who are still held fast in error and repent not, we have decreed and enjoined that they be put forth from the Church and be separated and removed from the faithful, because they are become heretics; and that the faithful be commanded wholly to avoid them, and not to communicate with them either in speech or in prayer. For these are enemies and spoilers of the Church; for concerning these our Lord commanded us and said to us: *Beware of the leaven of the Pharisees and of the Sadducees* (Mt. 16:6); and: *Into the cities of the Samaritans ye shall not enter* (Mt. 10:5). Now *the cities of the Samaritans* are those of the heresies, which go in a perverse way, concerning which He said in Proverbs: *There is a way which men think right: but the end thereof leadeth to the bottom of Sheol* (Prov. 14:12). These are they concerning whom our Lord sternly and bitterly gave sentence and said: *It shall not be forgiven them, neither in this world nor in the world to come* (Mt. 12:32). For as regards the People, who believed not in Christ and laid hands upon Him, it is against the Son of Man, on whom they laid hands, that they blaspheme; and our Lord said: *It shall be forgiven them* (Mt. 12:32); and again our Lord said of them: *My Father, they know not what they have done, nor what they speak: if it be possible, forgive them* (cf. Lk. 23:34; Mt. 26:39; 1 Tim. 1:7). And as for the Gentiles again, it is against the Son of Man also that they blaspheme, by reason of the cross; and for these there shall come forth forgiveness. For to those w ho have believed, from the People or from the Gentiles, forgiveness of their evil works has been granted through baptism; as the Lord Christ said: *Wherefore I say unto you: All sins and blasphemies shall be forgiven to men: but blasphemy against the Holy Spirit shall not be forgiven, neither in this world nor in the world to come. And everyone that shall say a word against the Son of Man, it shall be forgiven him; but everyone that shall say it against the Holy Spirit, it shall not be forgiven him, neither in this world nor in the world to come* (Mt. 12:31–32). But those who blaspheme the Holy Spirit, those who lightly and in hypocrisy blaspheme God Almighty, those heretics who receive not His holy Scriptures, or receive them ill, in hypocrisy with blaspheming, who with evil words blaspheme the Catholic Church which is the receptacle of the Holy Spirit: it is they who, before the judgement to come and before ever they can make a defence, are already condemned by Christ. For that which He said, *It shall not be forgiven them* (Mt. 12:32), is the stern sentence of condemnation which goes forth for them.

And when we had ordained and affirmed and set down these things together with one accord, we set forth to go each one to his former province, confirming the Churches. For those things which were foretold have been fulfilled, and the hidden wolves are come, the *false Christs and lying prophets* (Mt. 24:24; Mk. 13:22) have appeared. And this is evident and manifest, that when the times draw near and the Advent is at hand, there will be yet many more and worse than these: from whom the Lord God will deliver you.

Those then who have repented of the error of their godless apostasy we have healed with much admonition and with the word of doctrine and exhortation, and have made them whole and have suffered them to remain in the Churches; but those who are smitten unto death with the perverse word of error, and for whom there is no cure, we have driven out, that they may not contaminate the holy Catholic Church, the pure Church of God: that the evil may not creep like a leprosy and travel to all like a putrid gangrene, but that pure and without stain or blemish (cf. Eph. 5:27) or scar the Church may remain sound unto the Lord God. And these things we so do in every place and in every city, and throughout the whole world; and we have given our testimony, and have left this Catholic Didascalia justly and rightly to the Catholic Church for a memorial and for the confirming of the faithful.

Chapter XXVI

On the bonds of the Second Legislation of God.

But you who have been converted from the People to believe in God our Saviour Jesus Christ, do not henceforth continue in your former conversation, brethren, that you should keep vain obligations, purifications and sprinklings and baptisms and distinction of meats; for the Lord has said to you: *Remember not the former things;* and: *Behold, I make all things new: the which I now declare, that ye may know them. And I will make in the desert a way* (Isa. 43:18, 19). Now *deserts* the Churches formerly were, in which there is now a highway and the knowledge of religion, a way wherein there is no erring, but new and evident, even Jesus Christ and all His dispensation which was from the beginning. For you know that He gave a simple and pure and holy law, a law of life, wherein our Saviour set His name. For whereas He spoke the Ten Words, He signified Jesus: for Ten represents Yod; but Yod is the beginning of the name of Jesus. Now concerning the

Law the Lord testifies in David, saying thus: *The law of the Lord is without blemish, and converting souls* (Ps. 19:7 (18:7 LXX)). And many other things are said on this wise everywhere; for in completion of the writings of the Prophets the Lord spoke at the end by Malachi the Angel and said thus: *Remember the law of Moses the servant of the Lord, how he commanded you commandments and judgements* (Mal. 4:6). And our Saviour also, when He cleansed the leper, sent him to the Law, and said to him: *Go, show thyself to the high priests, and offer the gifts of thy cleansing, as Moses commanded, for a testimony unto them* (Mt. 8:4); that He might show that He does not undo the Law, but teaches what is the Law and what the Second Legislation. For He said thus: *I am not come to undo the law, nor the prophets, but to fulfil them* (Mt. 5:17). The Law therefore is indissoluble; but the Second Legislation is temporary, and is dissoluble. Now the Law consists of the Ten Words and the Judgements; to which Law Jesus bore witness and said thus: *One Yod letter shall not pass away from the law* (Mt. 5:18). Now it is the *Yod* which passes not away from the Law, even that which may be known from the Law itself through the Ten Words, which is the name of Jesus. But the *letter* is the extension of the wood of the cross. And in the mount also Moses and Elias appeared with our Lord: that is, the Law and the Prophets.

The Law then consists of the Ten Words and the Judgements, which God spoke before that the People made the calf and served idols. For also that it is called the Law, is truly on account of the Judgements. This is the simple and light Law, wherein is no burden, nor distinction of meats, nor incensings, nor offerings of sacrifices and burnt offerings. In this Law accordingly He shows concerning the dispensation of the Church and concerning the uncircumcision of the flesh only. For He spoke concerning sacrifices thus: *If thou shalt make me an altar, make it of earth: but if of stones, thou shalt make it of whole and unwrought, and not of wrought stones. Forasmuch as thou hast laid an iron tool upon it, thou hast also polluted it* (Ex. 20:24–25; Dt. 27:5–6)*:* not as speaking concerning the axe, but concerning the iron of the knife which is the physician's knife, with which he circumcises the foreskin. Wherefore He does not say, 'Make for me' but, *If thou shalt make an altar.* He did not impose this as a necessity, but showed what was about to be. For God had no need of sacrifices; as neither of old was it commanded Cain and Abel, but they of their own accord presented offerings: and their offering achieved a brother's murder. And Noah likewise offered, and was blamed. Wherefore He signified here: 'If thou desire to sacrifice, whereas I need it not thou sacrificest unto me.' So then the Law is easy and light, of no weak voice. But when the People denied God, who by Moses visited them in their afflictions, who wrought signs by his hand and through his rod, who smote the Egyptians with the ten plagues and divided the Red Sea in two, who led them in the midst of the sea on dry land as in the desert, who drowned their enemies and them that hated them, who with wood made sweet the fountain of the bitter waters of Marah, who made water to flow for them in abundance from the rock that they might be satisfied, who with a pillar of cloud and a pillar of fire overshadowed and guided them, who brought them down manna from heaven, and gave them flesh from the sea, who ordained the Law for them in the mount: Him they denied and said: *We have no God to go before us; and they made them a molten calf and worshipped it* (Ex. 32:1, 8) and sacrificed to a graven image. Therefore the Lord was angry; and in His hot anger — yet with the mercy of His goodness — He bound them with the Second Legislation, and laid heavy burdens upon them, and a hard yoke upon their neck. And He says now no longer: *If thou shalt make* (cf. Ex. 20:24–25; Dt. 27:5–6), as formerly; but He said: 'Make an altar, and sacrifice continually' as though He had need of these things. Wherefore He laid upon them continual burnt offerings with a necessity, and caused them to abstain from meats by means of distinctions of meats. For from that time were animals discerned, and clean and unclean flesh; from that time were separations, and purifications, and baptisms, and sprinklings; from that time were sacrifices, and offerings, and tables; from that time were burnt offerings, and oblations, and shewbread, and the offering up of sacrifices, and firstlings, and redemptions, and he-goats for sin, and vows, and many other things marvellous. For because of manifold sins there were laid upon them customs unspeakable; but by none of them did they abide, but they again provoked the Lord. Wherefore He yet added to them by the Second Legislation a blindness worthy of their works, and spoke thus: *If there be found in a man sins worthy of death, and he die, and ye hang him upon a tree; his body shall not remain the night upon the tree, but ye shall surely bury him the same day: for cursed is every one that is hanged upon a tree* (Dt. 21:22–23; cf. Gal. 3:13); that when Christ should come they might not be able to help Him, but might suppose that He was guilty of a curse. For their blinding therefore was this spoken, as Isaiah said: *Behold, I show my righteousness, and thine evils: and they shall not help thee at all* (Isa. 57:12). For the Lord judged them with a just judgement, and dealt thus with them because of their wickedness, and hardened their heart (cf. Jn. 12:40; Ex 4:21, etc.) like Pharaoh's; as the Lord said to them by Isaiah: *Hearing ye shall hear, and shall not understand; and seeing ye shall see, and shall not know. For the heart of this people is waxed gross; and their eyes they have shut, and their ears they have stopped, that they may not be converted: lest at any time they should see with their eyes, and hear with their ears* (Isa. 6:9–10; Acts 28:26–27). And in the Gospel again He said: *This people's heart is waxed gross; and their eyes they have shut, and their ears they have stopped, lest at any time they should be converted. But blessed are your eyes that see, and your ears that hear* (Mt. 13:15–16). For you have been released from the bonds, and relieved of the Second Legislation, and set free from bitter slavery, and the curse has been taken off and put away from you.

For the Second Legislation was imposed for the making of the calf and for idolatry. But you through baptism have been set free from idolatry, and from the Second Legislation, which was imposed on account of idols, you have been released. For in the Gospel He renewed and fulfilled and affirmed the Law; but the Second Legislation He did away and abolished. For indeed it was to this end that He came, that He might affirm the Law, and abolish the Second Legislation, and fulfil the power of men's liberty, and show forth the resurrection of the dead. For even before His coming He foretold His coming through the prophets, and together with His coming He signified also the disobedience of the People, and preached the undoing of the Second Legislation; as He said by Jeremiah: *Why bring ye me frankincense from Sheba, and cinnamon from a far country? Your burnt offerings are not acceptable unto me, and your sacrifices delight me not* (Jer. 6:20), And again He said: *Bring together your burnt offerings with your sacrifices, and eat flesh. For I gave you no command, when I brought you out from the land of Egypt, neither concerning burnt offerings nor concerning sacrifices* (Jer. 7:21–22). Yea, verily, in the Law He gave no command, but in the bonds of the Second Legislation, after that they had served idols. And again by Isaiah also He said: *To what purpose is the multitude of your sacrifices unto me? saith the Lord, I am sated with burnt offerings of rams; and the fat of lambs and the blood of oxen I desire not. And when ye come to see my face, who hath required these things at your hands? Trample my courts no more. If ye will bring me fine flour, it is a vain oblation; and your new moons and your sabbaths and solemn days are rejected of me: your fasts and your restings are not acceptable unto me, and your festivals my soul hateth* (Isa. 1:11–14). And in all the Scriptures He speaks thus; and through the sacrifices He abolishes the Second Legislation; for, as we have already said, it is in the Second Legislation that sacrifices are prescribed. If, then, even before His coming He made known and revealed His coming, and the disobedience of the People, and spoke of the abolition of the Second Legislation, much more, being come, did He fully and completely abolish the Second Legislation. For He did not use sprinklings, or baptisms, or other wonted rites; nor did He offer sacrifices or burnt offerings, or any thing that it is written in the Second Legislation to offer. And what else did He hereby signify but the abolition of the Second Legislation? as also He loosed you and called you from the bonds, and said: *Come unto me, all ye that toil and are laden with heavy burdens; and I will give you rest* (Mt. 11:28). Now we know that our Saviour did not say this to the Gentiles, but He said it to us His disciples from among the Jews, and brought us out from burdens and a heavy load.

Those therefore who do not obey Him, that He may lighten and deliver them from the bonds of the Second Legislation, obey not God, who has called them to come forth unto release and rest and refreshment; and they bind themselves with the heavy burdens of the Second Legislation, which are of no avail. For our Lord and Saviour Himself, who gave the Law and the Second Legislation, bears witness concerning the Law that it is life to them that keep it (Rom. 10:5; Lev. 18:5); but concerning the Second Legislation He testifies and shows that it is a bond and a blindness. For He everywhere makes a distinction; and He bears witness to the Law, and admonishes and commands us that we be under the Law: for every one who is not under law is lawless. And therefore He thus bears witness to the Law: *In the law of the Lord shall be his pleasure, and in his law will he meditate day and night. Not so the wicked* (Ps. 1:2). We see then, beloved, how the righteous are declared blessed on account of righteousness and the keeping of the Law. But *not so the wicked;* for they have no pleasure either in the righteous or in the Law, and they do not mediate therein. Wherefore He calls 'the wicked' those who do not converse according to the Law. For in the Gospel also He affirms the Law, and calls and brings us out from the burden of the bonds and from the Second Legislation. But that the Law is other than the Second Legislation, in David likewise He shows by a distinction, speaking thus: *Let us sever their cords, and loose their yoke from us* (Ps. 2:3). You see how the Holy Spirit speaks as it were out of the mouth of the world (cf. Acts 4:25) and reveals its thought, and says that the Law is a 'yoke' but the Second Legislation 'cords.' For the Law is a yoke, because like the plough-yoke of oxen it is laid upon the former People and upon the present Church of God; even as now in the Church it is upon us who are called from the People, and upon you who from among the Gentiles have obtained mercy: it has gathered and held us both together in one accord. But He well calls the Second Legislation 'bonds;' for when the People served idols, there was added to them the weight of the Second Legislation. For the bonds were justly imposed, as it befell the People then; but the Church has not been bound. For to Ezekiel He explains and makes known that the Law of life is one, but the second Law, of death, is another; for He spoke thus: *I brought them forth from the land of Egypt, and brought them into the wilderness, and gave them my commandments, and made known to them my judgements: that if a man should do them, he might live by them* (Ezek. 20:9–11). And afterwards, upbraiding them because they had sinned and had not kept the Law of life, He repeats to them and saith thus: *I have given them commandments that are not good, and judgements whereby they may not live* (Ezek. 20:25). Now the judgements which do not give life are those of the bonds. Hence also the word aforesaid in the Second Legislation was for the blinding of a blind people, to wit: *Cursed is everyone that is hanged upon a tree* (Dt. 21:23). For thus did they think of Him who gives and distributes blessings to them that are worthy, that He is under a curse. Wherefore, because they knew Him not, even after the signs that were done by Him in the world: when He suffered, justly in accordance with their works that word was set down for the blinding of the People; and it was a bar that they might not believe and be saved. Whence also by Isaiah He speaks thus: *Who is blind, but my servants? and the servants of God are blinded* (Isa. 42:19). *And I have brought out a blind people, that have eyes, and see not: and their ears also are deaf* (Isa. 43:8). For by this word, because of their works, their eyes were blinded, and their ears made deaf like Pharaoh's. Hence with this word the Second Legislation also was imposed, which Moses appointed. And it is the Second Legislation that He called *judgements that are not good* (Ezek. 20:25); and it cannot save alive.

They therefore who bring upon themselves those things which were imposed for the worship of idols, shall inherit the Woes; for *Woe to them that prolong their sins as a long rope, and their iniquity as the band of a heifer's yoke* (Isa. 5:18). For the yoke of the bonds is the *heifer's yoke* — the bonds of the Second Legislation now upon the People, which like *a long rope* is laid upon them by reason of other men's sins which from former times and generations they bring upon themselves. Everyone who strives to be under the Second Legislation becomes guilty of the calf-worship; for the Second Legislation was imposed for nothing else but for idolatry. For the bonds were decreed because of idolatry; they therefore who regard them are bondsmen and idolaters. Wherefore, every one who binds himself becomes guilty of the Woe, and ought likewise to profess idolatry. Now one who is such asserts also the curse against our Saviour; for if thou uphold the Second Legislation, thou also assertest the curse against our Saviour, and thou art held fast in the bonds and made guilty of the Woe — an enemy of the Lord God.

Cease therefore, beloved brethren, you who from among the People have believed, yet desire still to be tied with the bonds, and say that the Sabbath is prior to the first day of the week because that the Scripture has said: *In six days did God make all things; and on the seventh day he finished all his works, and he sanctified it* (Ex. 20:11; Gen. 2:2–3). We ask you now, which is first, Alaf or Tau? For that day which is the greater is that which is the beginning of the world, even as the Lord our Saviour said by Moses: *In the beginning God created the heaven and the earth. But the earth was invisible and unshapen* (Gen. 1:1–2). And again He said: *And there was one day* (Gen. 1:5): and as yet the seventh day was unknown. But what say you? Which is greater, that which had come into being, and existed, or that which was yet unknown, and of which there was no expectation that it should come to be? But again we ask you: Are your last children blessed, or the firstborn? as the Scripture also saith: *Jacob shall be blessed among the firstborn* (cf. Sir. 36:17); and: *My son, my firstborn is Israel* (Ex. 4:22); and: *Every male that openeth the womb of his mother is blessed to the Lord* (Lk. 2:23; cf. Ex. 13:2, 12).

But that we may make you firm in the faith, hear ye. The first day and the last are equal; for learn how you find it written, that *In his kingdom the day of the Lord is as a thousand years: the day of yesterday which is past; and as a watch of the night* (2 Pt. 3:8; cf. Ep. Barn. 15:4;

Ps. 90:4 (89:4 LXX)). One day therefore is a thousand years in the kingdom of Christ, wherein also will be the judgement. For *a watch of the night* He said concerning the judgement, which is a dark prison to them that are condemned. A day therefore is to be revealed in which the sun will stand in his mid-course, and the moon likewise, following the sun (cf. Hab. 3:11; Ep. Barn. 15:5). For He said: *Behold, I make the first things as the last, and the last as the first* (cf. Ep. Barn. 6:13)*;* and: *The last shall be first, and the first last* (Mt. 20:16)*;* and: *Remember no more the former things, and let them not come to your mind. Behold, I make things new, which now shall be revealed* (Isa. 43:18–19)*;* and: *In those days and in that time they shall no more say: The ark of the covenant; neither shall it come to mind, nor be visited, nor any more be made* (Jer. 3:16). But the Sabbath itself is counted even unto the Sabbath, and it becomes eight days; thus an ogdoad is reached, which is more than the Sabbath, even the first of the week.

Wherefore, brethren, every day is the Lord's; for the Scripture has said: *The earth is the Lord's with the fullness thereof: the world that is under heaven, and all that dwell therein* (Ps. 24:1 (23:1 LXX)). For if God willed that we should be idle one day for six, first of all the patriarchs and righteous men, and all they that were before Moses, would have remained idle upon it, and God Himself also with all His creatures. But now all the governance of the world is carried on ever continually; and the spheres do not cease even for a moment from their course, but at God's command their universal and perpetual motion proceeds. For if He would say: *Thou shalt be idle, and thy son, and thy servant, and thy maidservant, and thine ass* (cf. Ex. 20:10; Dt. 5:14), how does He continue to work, causing to generate, and making the winds to blow, and fostering and nourishing us His creatures? On the Sabbath day He causes the winds to blow, and the waters to flow, and thus works. But this the Sabbath has been set as a type for the times, even as many other things have been set for a type. The Sabbath therefore is a type of the final rest, signifying the seventh thousand years, But the Lord our Saviour, when He was come, fulfilled the types and explained the parables, and He showed those things that are life-giving, and those that cannot help He did away, and those that cannot give life He abolished.

And not only in His own person did He show this, but He wrought also by the Romans; and He overthrew the temple, and caused the altar to cease, and made an end of sacrifices, and all the commands and bonds that are in the Second Legislation He abolished, For the Romans also hold the Law, but they refuse the Second Legislation: therefore is their dominion strong. Thou, therefore, who desirest to-day to be under the Second Legislation, whilst the Romans rule thou canst not perform aught that is written in the Second Legislation. For thou canst not stone the wicked, nor kill idolaters, nor discharge the ministry of sacrifices, nor perform the libations and sprinklings with the ashes of a heifer (Num. 19:1–10; cf. Heb. 9:13); nor canst thou fulfil aught else of those things which are in the Second Legislation, nor observe them. For it is written: *Cursed is every one that keepeth not these words to do them* (Dt. 27:26; Gal 3:10)*;* and this is a thing impossible, to fulfil the Second Legislation while dispersed among the Gentiles. Wherefore, everyone that touches it falls under a curse, and binds himself, and inherits a Woe; and he asserts the curse against our Saviour, and as an enemy of God he is condemned.

But if thou follow Christ, thou shalt inherit the blessings (cf. 1 Pt. 3:9). For *there is no disciple better than his master* (Mt. 10:24)*:* but when thou conformest to Him, through the Gospel thou conformest to the Law, and thou wilt entirely avoid the Second Legislation: even as the Lord Himself, who gave the kingdom to men, declared also that His commands ought justly to be kept; for in every age there is of right a legislation given. Now having the Gospel, thou conformest to the Law, the renewal of the Law and the seal, beyond the Law and the Prophets seek nothing else. For the Second Legislation is undone, but the Law is made firm. And those who would be without the Law, against their will come under the Law; for He said in the Law: *Thou shalt not kill* (Ex. 20:13)*;* but if a man kill, he is condemned by the law of the Romans, and he comes under the Law. But if you follow and conform to the truth of the Church and the power of the Gospel, your hope in the Lord shall not be frustrated.

Do you therefore avoid all heretics, who follow not the Law and the Prophets, and obey not Almighty God, but are His enemies; and who abstain from meats, and forbid to marry, and believe not in the resurrection of the body; who moreover will not eat and drink, but would fain rise up demons, unsubstantial spirits, who shall be damned everlastingly and punished in unquenchable fire. Fly and avoid them therefore, that you may not perish with them.

But if there be any who are precise and desire, after the Second Legislation, to observe the wonted courses of nature and issues and marriage intercourse: first let them know that, as we have already said, together with the Second Legislation they affirm the curse against our Saviour and condemn themselves to no purpose. And again, let them tell us, in what days or in what hours they keep themselves from prayer and from receiving the Eucharist, or from reading the Scriptures — let them tell us whether they are void of the Holy Spirit. For through baptism they receive the Holy Spirit, who is ever with those that work righteousness, and does not depart from them by reason of natural issues and the intercourse of marriage, but is ever and always with those who possess Him, and keeps them; as the Lord said in Proverbs: *If thou sleep. he keepeth thee; and when thou awakest, he will speak with thee* (Prov. 6:22). And in the Gospel also our Lord said: *Everyone that hath, there shall be given to him, and shall be added unto him; but from him that hath not, even that which he thinketh he hath shall be taken away* (Lk. 8:18 (Mt. 8:12, 25.29; Mk. 4:25)). To those therefore who have, yea, it shall be added unto them; but from those who think that they have not, even that which they think they have shall be taken away.

For if thou think, O woman, that in the seven days of thy flux thou art void of the Holy Spirit; if thou die in those days, thou wilt depart empty and without hope. But if the Holy Spirit is always in thee, without just impediment dost thou keep thyself from prayer and from the Scriptures and from the Eucharist. For consider and see, that prayer also is heard through the Holy Spirit, and the Eucharist through the Holy Spirit is accepted and sanctified, and the Scriptures are the words of the Holy Spirit, and are holy. For if the Holy Spirit is in thee, why dost thou keep thyself from approaching to the works of the Holy Spirit? as those who say: *Whosoever sweareth by the altar, sinneth not; but whosoever sweareth by the gift that is upon it, sinneth.* As our Lord said: *Fools and blind, whether is greater, the gift, or the altar that sanctifieth the gift? Everyone therefore that sweareth by the altar, sweareth by it, and by all that is upon it, And every one that sweareth by the temple, sweareth by it, and by him that dwelleth therein. And every one that sweareth by the heaven, sweareth by the throne of God, and by him that sitteth thereon* (Mt. 23:18–22).

If therefore thou possess the Holy Spirit, but keep thyself from His fruits so that thou approach not to them, thou also shalt hear from our Lord Jesus Christ: 'Fool and blind, whether is greater, the bread, or the Spirit that sanctifieth the bread?' Therefore, if the Holy Spirit thou possessest: fool, thou keepest vain observances. But if the Holy Spirit is not in thee, how canst thou work righteousness? For the Holy Spirit continues ever with those who possess Him; but from whom He departs, to him an unclean spirit joins himself. *For the unclean spirit, when he is gone out from a man, departeth and goeth about in waterless places* — that is, men who go not down into the water of baptism — and *when he hath found him no rest, he saith: I will return to my former house, whence I came out. If therefore he come and find it empty and swept and garnished, then he goeth and taketh with him seven other spirits worse than himself, and they come and dwell in that man; and his last state is made worse than the first* (Mt. 12:43–45).

Learn now, why, when the unclean spirit is gone out, he finds him no rest in any place: because every man soever is filled with a spirit, one with the Holy Spirit, and one with an unclean spirit. A believer is filled with the Holy Spirit, and an unbeliever with an unclean spirit: and his nature does not receive an alien spirit. He therefore who has withdrawn and separated himself and departed from the unclean spirit by baptism, is filled with the Holy Spirit; and if he do good works, the Holy Spirit continues with him, and he remains fulfilled; and the unclean spirit finds no place with him, for he who is filled with the Holy Spirit does not receive him. For all men are filled with their own spirit; and the unclean spirits depart not even a little from the heathen, while yet they are heathens, even though they imagine that they do good works; for there is no other power whereby the unclean spirit may depart save by the pure and holy Spirit of God. Thus, then, when he has nowhere found him a place to enter, he returns and comes to him from whom he went forth; because one who is filled with the Holy Spirit does not receive him.

Thou then, O woman, according as thou sayest, if in the days of thy flux thou art void, thou shalt be filled with unclean spirits. For when the unclean spirit returns to thee and finds him a place, he will enter and dwell in thee always: and then will there be entering in of the unclean spirit and going forth of the Holy Spirit, and perpetual warfare. Wherefore, O foolish women, these misfortunes befall you because of your imaginings; and because of the observances which you keep, and on account of your imaginings, you are emptied of the Holy Spirit and filled with unclean spirits: and you are cast out from life into the burning of everlasting fire. But again I will say to thee, O woman: In the seven days of thy flux thou accountest thyself unclean according to the Second Legislation: after seven days, therefore, how canst thou be cleansed without baptism? But if thou be baptized for that which thou supposest, thou wilt undo the perfect baptism of God which wholly forgave thee thy sins, and wilt be found in the evil plight of thy former sins; and thou shalt be delivered over to eternal fire. But if thou be not baptized, according to thine own supposition thou remainest unclean, and the vain observing of the seven days has availed thee nothing, but is rather hurtful to thee; for according to thy supposition thou art unclean, and as unclean thou shalt be condemned.

Be thus minded therefore concerning all those who observe issues and the intercourse of marriage; for all these observances are foolish and hurtful. For if, when a man use matrimony, or a blood come forth from him, he be baptized, let him also wash his couch: and he will have this labour and vexation incessantly; he will be baptizing and will be washing his clothes and his couch, and will be able to do nothing else. Now if thou be baptized from an issue and from marriage intercourse according to the Second Legislation, thou owest it also to be baptized when thou treadest upon a mouse: and thou shalt never be clean. For even as to the shoes of thy feet, with the skin of dead animals and with the hides of those that are sacrificed thou art shod; and as to clothes also, with the wool of the like animals thou art clothed. And if thou tread upon a bone, or enter a tomb, thou oughtest to be baptized: and thou shalt never be clean. And thou wilt undo the baptism of God, and thou renewest thy offences, and art found in thy former sins, and affirmest the Second Legislation, and takest upon thee the idolatry of the calf, — for if thou take upon thee the Second Legislation, take also idolatry, for because of idolatry the Second Legislation was imposed, — and the former sins of others, *as a long rope, and as the band of a heifer* (Isa 5.18)*;* thou drawest and bringest upon thee. Moreover, thou bringest upon thee the Woe; for when thou affirmest the Second Legislation, thou consentest to the curse against our Saviour; and thou settest at naught Christ the King, who distributes blessings to them that are worthy. Wherefore thou shalt inherit a curse; for *every one that shall curse a man is cursed and every one that blesseth is blessed* (cf. Num. 24:9). To what curses, therefore, and to what judgement or to what condemnation shall they be delivered who affirm a curse against our Saviour and our Lord and our God!

Wherefore, beloved, flee and avoid such observances: for you have received release, that you should no more bind yourselves; and do not load yourselves again with that which our Lord and Saviour has lifted from you. And do not observe these things, nor think them uncleanness; and do not refrain yourselves on their account, nor seek after sprinklings, or baptisms, or purification for these things. For in the Second Legislation, if one touch a dead man or a tomb, he is baptized; but do you, according to the Gospel and according to the power of the Holy Spirit, come together even in the cemeteries, and read the holy Scriptures, and without demur perform your ministry and your supplication to God; and offer an acceptable Eucharist, the likeness of the royal body of Christ, both in your congregations and in your cemeteries and on the departures of them that sleep — pure bread that is made with fire and sanctified with invocations — and without doubting pray and offer for them that are fallen asleep. For they who have believed in God, according to the Gospel, even though they should sleep, they are not dead (cf. Jn. 11:25); as our Lord said to the Sadducees: *Concerning the resurrection of the dead, have ye not read that which is written: I am the God of Abraham, and the God of Isaac, and the God of Jacob? And he is not the God of the dead, but of the living* (Mt. 22:31–33). And Elisha the prophet also, after he had slept and was a long while dead, raised up a dead man; for his body touched the body of the dead and quickened and raised it up (2 Kgs. 13:21). But this could not have been were it not that, even when he was fallen asleep, his body was holy and filled with the Holy Spirit.

For this cause therefore do you approach without restraint to those who are at rest, and hold them not unclean. In like manner also you shall not separate those women who are in the wonted courses; for she also who had the flow of blood was not chidden when she touched the skirt of our Saviour's cloak, but was even vouchsafed the forgiveness of all her sins (Mt. 9:20–22). And when your wives suffer those issues which are according to nature, have a care that, in a manner that is right, you cleave to them; for you know that they are your members, and do you love them as your soul: as it is written in the Twelve Prophets, in Malachi who was called the Angel: *The Lord hath borne witness between thee and the wife of thy youth, whom thou hast left, thy partner, and she the wife of thy covenant. And did not he make her? and they are the residue of his spirit. And ye have said: What else doth God seek but pure seed? Give heed in your spirits: and the wife of thy youth thou shalt not leave* (Mal. 2:14–15). Wherefore, a woman when she is in the way of women, and a man when an issue comes forth from him, and a man and his wife when they consort and rise up one from another: let them assemble without restraint, without bathing, for they are clean. But if a man should corrupt and defile another's wife after baptism, or be polluted with a harlot, and rising up from her should bathe in all the seas and oceans and be baptized in all the rivers, he cannot be made clean.

Do you therefore, our beloved, avoid all such foolish observances, and come not near them. And be careful to abide in the wedded company of one wife, and to keep your bodies unspotted and unsullied; that you may receive life, that you may be partakers of the kingdom of God, and that you may receive that which the

Lord God has promised, and may have rest for evermore.

Now with many other demonstrations similar to these we might the more clearly declare to you the Didascalia; but not to extend and prolong the writing, already we conclude the discourse and lay it aside, lest by reason of the severity of the truth the teaching of our discourse should remain but a short time with you. Wherefore, take not amiss those things which have been said; for our Lord and Saviour also spoke with severity to those who were worthy of condemnation, and said: *Take and cast them into the outer darkness: there shall be weeping and gnashing of teeth* (Mt. 25:30); and: *Depart from me, ye cursed, into everlasting fire, which my Father hath prepared for the evil one and his angels* (Mt. 25:41). That the word is likened to fire and a sword, He has said also in Jeremiah: *Behold, my words go forth as fire, and as iron that cutteth stone* (Jer. 23:29)— yet sword and fire and constraint, not to those who hearken to the truth, but He means that word which the People heard not with pleasure when our Lord and Teacher reproved them; for they were unwilling to hearken to it because they esteemed it hard like iron. For they hearkened not to that which He said to them, for He appeared to them to speak harshly and severely. Wherefore He said to them: *Why call ye me Lord, Lord, and that which I say ye do not?* (Lk. 6:46) And so in like manner this our writing also appears to some to speak harshly and severely by reason of its truth. For if we had written indulgently for the gratification of men, many would grow weak and melt away from the faith, and we should be guilty of their blood. For as a physician, when he has not been able to conquer and heal an ulcer with drugs and fomentations, comes to a severer remedy and to surgical cuttings, that is to iron and cauteries, by which alone the physician is able to overcome and conquer the sore and presently heal the sick man: even so is the word; to those who hear and do it it is as a compress and an emollient and a plaster, but by those who hear and do it not it is esteemed as iron and fire.

Now to Him who is able to open the ears of your hearts (cf. Rom. 16:25; 2 Mac. 1:4) to receive the incisive words of the Lord through the Gospel and the teaching of Jesus Christ the Nazarene, who was crucified in the days of Pontius Pilate, and slept, that He might announce to Abraham and to Isaac and to Jacob and to all His saints the end of the world and the resurrection that is to be for the dead; and rose from the dead, that He might show and give to us, that we might know Him, a pledge of the resurrection; and was taken up to heaven by the power of God His Father and of the Holy Spirit, and sat on the right hand of the throne of God Almighty upon the Cherubim; to Him who cometh with power and glory to judge the dead and the living: to Him be dominion and glory and majesty and kingdom, and to His Father and to the Holy Spirit: who was, and is, and abideth, both now and unto all generations and ages.

Amen.

Apostolic Tradition

Traditionally attributed to Hippolytus (early 3rd century)

Part I

Let the bishop be ordained after he has been chosen by all the people. When he has been named and shall please all, let him, with the presbytery and such bishops as may be present, assemble with the people on a Sunday. While all give their consent, the bishops shall lay their hands upon him, and the presbytery shall stand by in silence. All indeed shall keep silent, praying in their heart for the descent of the Spirit. Then one of the bishops who are present shall, at the request of all, lay his hand on him who is ordained bishop, and shall pray as follows, saying:

God and Father of our Lord Jesus Christ, Father of mercies and God of all comfort, who dwellest on high yet hast respect to the lowly, who knowest all things before they come to pass. Thou hast appointed the borders of thy church by the word of thy grace, predestinating from the beginning the righteous race of Abraham. [3]And making them princes and priests, and leaving not thy sanctuary without a ministry, thou hast from the beginning of the world been well pleased to be glorified among those whom thou hast chosen. Pour forth now that power, which is thine, of thy royal Spirit, which thou gavest to thy beloved Servant Jesus Christ, which he bestowed on his holy apostles, who established the church in every place, the church which thou hast sanctified unto unceasing glory and praise of thy name. Thou who knowest the hearts of all, grant to this thy servant, whom thou hast chosen to be bishop, (to feed thy holy flock and to serve as thy high priest without blame, ministering night and day, to propitiate thy countenance without ceasing and to offer thee the gifts of thy holy church. And by the Spirit of high-priesthood to have authority to remit sins according to thy commandment, to assign the lots according to thy precept, to loose every bond according to the authority which thou gavest to thy apostles, and to please thee in meekness and purity of heart, offering to thee an odour of sweet savour. Through thy Servant Jesus Christ our Lord, through whom be to thee glory, might, honour, with the Holy Spirit in the holy church, both now and always and world without end. Amen.

And when he is made bishop, all shall offer him the kiss of peace, for he has been made worthy. [2]To him then the deacons shall bring the offering, and he, laying his hand upon it, with all the presbytery, shall say as the thanksgiving:

The Lord be with you.

And all shall say
And with thy spirit.

Lift up your hearts.
We lift them up unto the Lord.

Let us give thanks to the Lord.
It is meet and right.

And then he shall proceed immediately:

We give thee thanks, O God, through thy beloved Servant Jesus Christ, whom at the end of time thou didst send to us a Saviour and Redeemer and the Messenger of thy counsel. Who is thy Word, inseparable from thee; through whom thou didst make all things and in whom thou art well pleased. Whom thou didst send from heaven into the womb of the Virgin, and who, dwelling within her, was made flesh, and was manifested as thy Son, being born of the Holy Spirit and the Virgin. Who, fulfilling thy will, and winning for himself a holy people, spread out his hands when he came to suffer, that by his death he might set free them who believed on thee. Who, when he was betrayed to his willing death, that he might bring to nought death, and break the bonds of the devil, and tread hell under foot, and give light to the righteous, and set up a boundary post, and manifest his resurrection, taking bread and giving thanks to thee said: Take, eat: this is my body, which is broken for you. And likewise also the cup, saying: This is my blood, which is shed for you. As often as ye perform this, perform my memorial.

Having in memory, therefore, his death and resurrection, we offer to thee the bread and the cup, yielding thee thanks, because thou hast counted us worthy to stand before thee and to minister to thee.

And we pray thee that thou wouldest send thy Holy Spirit upon the offerings of thy holy church; that thou, gathering them into one, wouldest grant to all thy saints who partake to be filled with the Holy Spirit, that their faith may be confirmed in truth, that we may praise and glorify thee. Through thy Servant Jesus

Christ, through whom be to thee glory and honour, with the Holy Spirit in the holy church, both now and always and world without end. Amen.

If anyone offers oil, he shall give thanks as at the offering of the bread and wine, though not with the same words but in the same general manner, saying:

That sanctifying this oil, O God, wherewith thou didst anoint kings, priests and prophets, thou wouldest grant health to them who use it and partake of it, so that it may bestow comfort on all who taste it and health on all who use it.

Likewise, if anyone offers cheese and olives, let him say thus:

Sanctify this milk that has been united into one mass, and unite us to thy love. Let thy loving kindness ever rest upon this fruit of the olive, which is a type of thy bounty, which thou didst cause to flow from the tree unto life for them who hope on thee.

But at every blessing shall be said:

Glory be to thee, with the Holy Spirit in the holy church, both now and always and world without end. Amen.

But when a presbyter is ordained, the bishop shall lay his hand upon his head, while the presbyters touch him, and he shall say according to those things that were said above, as we have prescribed above concerning the bishop, praying and saying:

God and Father of our Lord Jesus Christ, look upon this thy servant, and grant to him the Spirit of grace and counsel of a presbyter, that he may sustain and govern thy people with a pure heart; [3]as thou didst look upon thy chosen people and didst command Moses that he should choose presbyters, whom thou didst fill with thy Spirit, which thou gavest to thy servant. And now, O Lord, grant that there may be unfailingly preserved amongst us the Spirit of thy grace, and make us worthy that, believing, we may minister to thee in simplicity of heart, praising thee. Through thy Servant Jesus Christ, through whom be to thee glory and honour, with the Holy Spirit in the holy church, both now and always and world without end. Amen.

But the deacon, when he is ordained, is chosen according to those things that were said above, the bishop alone in like manner laying his hands upon him, as we have prescribed. When the deacon is ordained, this is the reason why the bishop alone shall lay his hands upon him: he is not ordained to the priesthood but to serve the bishop and to carry out the bishop's commands. He does not take part in the council of the clergy; he is to attend to his own duties and to make known to the bishop such things as are needful. He does not receive that Spirit that is possessed by the presbytery, in which the presbyters share; he receives only what is confided in him under the bishop's authority.

For this cause the bishop alone shall make a deacon. But on a presbyter, however, the presbyters shall lay their hands because of the common and like Spirit of the clergy. Yet the presbyter has only the power to receive; but he has no power to give. For this reason a presbyter does not ordain the clergy; but at the ordination of a presbyter he seals while the bishop ordains.

Over a deacon, then, he shall say as follows:

O God, who hast created all things and hast ordered them by thy Word, the Father of our Lord Jesus Christ, whom thou didst send to minister thy will and to manifest to us thy desire; grant the Holy Spirit of grace and care and diligence to this thy servant, whom thou hast chosen to serve the church and to offer in thy holy sanctuary the gifts that are offered to thee by thine appointed high priests, so that serving without blame and with a pure heart he may be counted worthy of this exalted office, by thy goodwill, praising thee continually. Through thy Servant Jesus Christ, through whom be to thee glory and honour, with the Holy Spirit, in the holy church, both now and always and world without end. Amen.

On a confessor, if he has been in bonds for the name of the Lord, hands shall not be laid for the diaconate or the presbyterate, for he has the honour of the presbyterate by his confession. But if he is to be ordained bishop, hands shall be laid upon him.

But if he is a confessor who was not brought before the authorities nor was punished with bonds nor was shut up in prison, but was insulted casually or privately for the name of the Lord, even though he confessed, hands are to be laid upon him for every office of which he is worthy.

The bishop shall give thanks (in all ordinations) as we have prescribed. It is not, to be sure, necessary for anyone to recite the exact words that we have prescribed, by learning to say them by heart in his thanksgiving to God; but let each one pray according to his ability. If, indeed, he is able to pray competently with an elevated prayer, it is well. But even if he is only moderately able to pray and give praise, no one may forbid him; only let him pray sound in the faith.

When a widow is appointed, she shall not be ordained but she shall be appointed by the name. If her husband has been long dead, she may be appointed (without delay). But if her husband has died recently, she shall not be trusted; even if she is aged she must be tested by time, for often the passions grow old in those who yield to them.

The widow shall be appointed by the word alone, and (so) she shall be associated with the other widows; hands shall not be laid upon her because she does not offer the oblation nor has she a sacred ministry. Ordination is for the clergy on account of their ministry, but the widow is appointed for prayer, and prayer is the duty of all.

The reader is appointed by the bishop's giving him the book, for he is not ordained.

Hands shall not be laid upon a virgin, for it is her purpose alone that makes her a virgin.

Hands shall not be laid upon a subdeacon, but his name shall be mentioned that he may serve the deacon.

If anyone says, "I have received the gift of healing", hands shall not be laid upon him: the deed shall make manifest if he speaks the truth.

Part II

New converts to the faith, who are to be admitted as hearers of the word, shall first be brought to the teachers before the people assemble. And they shall be examined as to their reason for embracing the faith, and they who bring them shall testify that they are competent to hear the word. Inquiry shall then be made as to the nature of their life; whether a man has a wife or is a slave. If he is the slave of a believer and he has his master's permission, then let him be received; but if his master does not give him a good character, let him be rejected. If his master is a heathen, let the slave be taught to please his master, that the word be not blasphemed. If a man has a wife or a woman a husband, let the man be instructed to content himself with his wife and the woman to content herself with her husband. But if a man is unmarried, let him be instructed to abstain from impurity, either by lawfully marrying a wife or else by remaining as he is. But if any man is possessed with demons, he shall not be admitted as a bearer until he is cleansed.

Inquiry shall likewise be made about the professions and trades of those who are brought to be admitted to the faith. If a man is a pander, he must desist or be rejected. If a man is a sculptor or painter, he must be charged not to make idols; if he does not desist he must be rejected. If a man is an actor or pantomimist, he must desist or be rejected. A teacher of young children had best desist, but if he has no other occupation, he may be permitted to continue. A charioteer, likewise, who races or frequents races, must desist or be rejected. A gladiator or a trainer of gladiators, or a huntsman (in the wild-beast shows), or anyone connected with these shows, or a public official in charge of gladiatorial exhibitions must desist or be rejected. A heathen priest or anyone who tends idols must desist or be rejected. A soldier of the civil authority must be taught not to kill men and to refuse to do so if he is commanded, and to refuse to take an oath; if he is unwilling to comply, he must be rejected. A military commander or civic magistrate that wears the purple must resign or be rejected. If a catechumen or a believer seeks to become a soldier, they must be rejected, for they have despised God. A harlot or licentious man or one who has castrated himself, or any other who does things not to be named, must be rejected, for they are defiled. A magician must not (even) be brought for examination. An enchanter, an astrologer, a diviner, a soothsayer, a user of magic verses, a juggler, a mountebank, an amulet-maker must desist or be rejected. A concubine, who is a slave and has reared her children and has been faithful to her master alone, may become a hearer; but if she has failed in these matters she must be rejected. If a man has a concubine, he must desist and marry legally; if he is unwilling, he must be rejected.

If, now, we have omitted anything, the facts (as they occur) will instruct your mind; for we all have the Spirit of God.

Let catechumens spend three years as hearers of the word. But if a man is zealous and perseveres well in the work, it is not the time but his character that is decisive.

When the teacher finishes his instruction, the catechumens shall pray by themselves, apart from the believers. And (all) women, whether believers or catechumens, shall stand for their prayers by themselves in a separate part of the church.

And when (the catechumens) finish their prayers, they must not give the kiss of peace, for their kiss is not yet pure. Only believers shall salute one another, but men with men and women with women; a man shall not salute a woman.

And let all the women have their heads covered with an opaque cloth, not with a veil of thin linen, for this is not a true covering.

At the close of their prayer, when their instructor lays his hand upon the catechumens, he shall pray and dismiss them; whoever gives the instruction is to do this, whether a cleric or a layman.

If a catechumen should be arrested for the name of the Lord, let him not hesitate about bearing his testimony; for if it should happen that they treat him shamefully and kill him, he will be justified, for he has been baptized in his own blood.

They who are to be set apart for baptism shall be chosen after their lives have been examined: whether they have lived soberly, whether they have honoured the widows, whether they have visited the sick, whether they have been active in well-doing. When their sponsors have testified that they have done these things, then let them hear the Gospel. Then from the time that they are separated from the other catechumens, hands shall be laid upon them daily in exorcism and, as the day of their baptism draws near, the bishop himself shall exorcise each one of them that he may be personally assured of their purity. Then, if there is any of them who is not good or pure, he shall be put aside as not having heard the word in faith; for it is never possible for the alien to be concealed.

Then those who are set apart for baptism shall be instructed to bathe and free themselves from impurity and wash themselves on Thursday. If a woman is menstruous, she shall be set aside and baptized on some other day.

They who are to be baptized shall fast on Friday, and on Saturday the bishop shall assemble them and command them to kneel in prayer. And, laying his hand upon them, he shall exorcise all evil spirits to flee away and never to return; when he has done this he shall breathe in their faces, seal their foreheads, ears and noses, and then raise them up. They shall spend all that night in vigil, listening to reading and instruction.

They who are to be baptized shall bring with them no other vessels than the one each will bring for the eucharist; for it is fitting that he who is counted worthy of baptism should bring his offering at that time.

At cockcrow prayer shall be made over the water. The stream shall flow through the baptismal tank or pour into it from above when there is no scarcity of water; but if there is a scarcity, whether constant or sudden, then use whatever water you can find.

They shall remove their clothing. And first baptize the little ones; if they can speak for themselves, they shall do so; if not, their parents or other relatives shall speak for them. Then baptize the men, and last of all the women; they must first loosen their hair and put aside any gold or silver ornaments that they were wearing: let no one take any alien thing down to the water with them.

At the hour set for the baptism the bishop shall give thanks over oil and put it into a vessel: this is called the "oil of thanksgiving". And he shall take other oil and exorcise it: this is called "the oil of exorcism". (The anointing is performed by a presbyter.) A deacon shall bring the oil of exorcism, and shall stand at the presbyter's left hand; and another deacon shall take the oil of thanksgiving, and shall stand at the presbyter's right hand. Then the presbyter, taking hold of each of those about to be baptized, shall command him to renounce, saying:

I renounce thee, Satan, and all thy servants and all thy works.

And when he has renounced all these, the presbyter shall anoint him with the oil of exorcism, saying:

Let all spirits depart far from thee.

Then, after these things, let him give him over to the presbyter who baptizes, and let the candidates stand in the water, naked, a deacon going with them likewise. And when he who is being baptized goes down into the water, he who baptizes him, putting his hand on him, shall say thus:

Dost thou believe in God, the Father Almighty?

And he who is being baptized shall say:

I believe.

Then holding his hand placed on his head, he shall baptize him once. And then he shall say:

Dost thou believe in Christ Jesus, the Son of God, who was born of the Holy Ghost of the Virgin Mary, and was crucified under Pontius Pilate, and was dead and buried, and rose again the third day, alive from the dead, and ascended into heaven, and sat at the right hand of the Father, and will come to judge the quick and the dead? And when he says:

I believe,

he is baptized again. And again he shall say:

Dost thou believe in the Holy Ghost, and the holy church, and the resurrection of the flesh?

He who is being baptized shall say accordingly:

I believe,

and so he is baptized a third time.

And afterward, when he has come up (out of the water), he is anointed by the presbyter with the oil of thanksgiving, the presbyter saying:

I anoint thee with holy oil in the name of Jesus Christ.

And so each one, after drying himself, is immediately clothed, and then is brought into the church.

Then the bishop, laying his hand upon them, shall pray, saying:

O Lord God, who hast made them worthy to obtain remission of sins through the laver of regeneration of the Holy Spirit, send into them thy grace, that they may serve thee according to thy will; for thine is the glory, to the Father and the Son, with the Holy Spirit in the holy church, both now and world without end. Amen.

Then, pouring the oil of thanksgiving from his hand and putting it on his forehead, he shall say:

I anoint thee with holy oil in the Lord, the Father Almighty and Christ Jesus and the Holy Ghost.

And signing them on the forehead he shall say:

The Lord be with thee;

and he who is signed shall say:

And with thy spirit.

And so he shall do to each one.

And immediately thereafter they shall join in prayer with all the people, but they shall not pray with the faithful until all these things are completed. And at the close of their prayer they shall give the kiss of peace.

And then the offering is immediately brought by the deacons to the bishop, and by thanksgiving he shall make the bread into an image of the body of Christ, and the cup of wine mixed with water according to the likeness of the blood, which is shed for all who believe in him. And milk and honey mixed together for the fulfilment of the promise to the fathers, which spoke of a land flowing with milk and honey; namely, Christ's flesh which he gave, by which they who believe are nourished like babes, he making sweet the bitter things of the heart by the gentleness of his word. And the water into an offering in a token of the laver, in order that the inner part of man, which is a living soul, may receive the same as the body.

The bishop shall explain the reason of all these things to those who partake. And when he breaks the bread and distributes the fragments he shall say:

The heavenly bread in Christ Jesus.

And the recipient shall say, Amen.

And the presbyters—or if there are not enough presbyters, the deacons—shall hold the cups, and shall stand by with reverence and modesty; first he who holds the water, then the milk, thirdly the wine. And the recipients shall taste of each three times, he who gives the cup saying:

In God the Father Almighty;

and the recipient shall say, Amen. Then:

In the Lord Jesus Christ;

and he shall say, Amen. Then:

In the Holy Ghost and the holy church;

and he shall say, Amen. So it shall be done to each.

And when these things are completed, let each one hasten to do good works, and to please God and to live aright, devoting himself to the church, practising the things he has learned, advancing in the service of God.

Now we have briefly delivered to you these things concerning the holy baptism and the holy oblation, for you have already been instructed concerning the resurrection of the flesh and all other things as taught in Scripture. Yet if there is any other thing that ought to be told (to converts), let the bishop impart it to them privately after their baptism; let not unbelievers know it, until they are baptized: this is the white stone of which John said: "There is upon it a new name written, which no one knoweth but he that receiveth the stone".

Part III

Widows and virgins shall fast frequently and shall pray for the church; presbyters, if they wish, and laymen may fast likewise. But the bishop may fast only when all the people fast.

For it constantly happens that some one wishes to make an offering—and such a one must not be denied—and then the bishop, after breaking the bread, must in every case taste and eat it with the other believers. (At such an offering) each shall take from the bishop's hand a piece of (this) bread before breaking his own bread. (This service has a special ceremonial) for it is "a Blessing", not "a Thanksgiving", as is (the service of) the Body of the Lord. But before drinking, each one, as many of you as are present, must take a cup and give thanks over it, and so go to your meal.

But to the catechumens is given exorcised bread, and each of them must offer the cup. No catechumen shall sit at the Lord's Supper.

But at each act of offering, the offerer must remember his host, for he was invited to the latter's home for that very purpose. But when you eat and drink, do so in an orderly manner and not so that anyone may mock, or your host be saddened by your unruliness, but behave so that he may pray to be made worthy that the saints may enter his dwelling: "for ye", it is said, "are the salt of the earth".

If the offering should be one made to all the guests jointly, take your portion from your host (and depart). But if all are to eat then and there, do not eat to excess, so that your host may likewise send some of what the saints leave to whomsoever he will and (so) may rejoice in the faith.

But while the guests are eating, let them eat silently, not arguing, (attending to) such things as the bishop may teach, but if he should ask any question, let an answer be given him; and when he says anything, everyone in modest praise shall keep silence until he asks again.

And even if the bishop should be absent when the faithful meet at a supper, if a presbyter or a deacon is present they shall eat in a similar orderly fashion, and each shall be careful to take the blessed bread from the presbyter's or deacon's hand; and in the same way the catechumens shall take the same exorcised bread.

But if (only) laymen meet, let them not act presumptuously, for a layman cannot bless the blessed bread.

Let each one eat in the name of the Lord; for this is pleasing to the Lord that we should be jealous (of our good name) even among the heathen, all sober alike.

If anyone wishes to give a meal to widows of mature years, let him dismiss them before evening. But if, on account of existing conditions, he cannot (feed them in his house), let him send them away, and they may eat of his food at their homes in any way they please.

As soon as first-fruits appear, all shall hasten to offer them to the bishop. And he shall offer them, shall give thanks and shall name him who offered them, saying:

We give thee thanks, O God, and we offer thee the first-fruits; which thou hast given us to enjoy, nourishing them through thy word, commanding the earth to bring forth her fruits for the gladness and the food of men and all beasts. For all these things we praise thee, O God, and for all things wherewith thou hast blessed us, who for us adornest every creature with divers fruits. Through thy Servant Jesus Christ, our Lord, through whom be to thee glory, world without end. Amen.

Only certain fruits may be blessed, namely grapes, the fig, the pomegranate, the olive, the pear, the apple, the mulberry, the peach, the cherry, the almond, the plum. Not the pumpkin, nor the melon, nor the cucumber, nor the onion nor garlic nor anything else having an odour.

But sometimes flowers too are offered; here the rose and the lily may be offered, but no other.

But for everything that is eaten shall they (who eat it) give thanks to the Holy God, eating unto His glory.

Let no one at the paschal season eat before the offering is made, otherwise he shall not be credited with the fast. But if any woman is with child, or if anyone is sick and cannot fast for two days, let such a one, on account of his need, (at least) fast on Saturday, contenting himself with bread and water. But if anyone on a voyage or for any other necessary cause should not know the day, when he has learned the truth he shall postpone his fast until after Pentecost. For the ancient type has passed away, and so the (postponed) fast (of Numbers 9. 11) in the second month has ceased, and each one ought to fast in accord with his knowledge of the truth.

Each of the deacons, with the subdeacons, shall be alert on the bishop's behalf, for the bishop must be informed if any are sick so that, if he pleases, he may visit them; for a sick man is greatly comforted when the high priest is mindful of him.

Let the deacons and the presbyters assemble daily at the place which the bishop may appoint; let the deacons (in particular) never fail to assemble unless prevented by sickness. When all have met they shall instruct those who are in the church, and then, after prayer, each shall go to his appointed duties.

No exorbitant charge shall be made for burial in the cemetery, for it belongs to all the poor; only the hire of the grave-digger and the cost of the tile (for closing the niche in the catacombs) shall be asked. The wages of the caretakers are to be paid by the bishop, lest any of those who go to that place be burdened (with a charge).

Part IV

Let all the faithful, whether men or women, when early in the morning they rise from their sleep and before they undertake any tasks, wash their hands and pray to God; and so they may go to their duties. But if any instruction in God's word is held (that day), everyone ought to attend it willingly, recollecting that he will hear God speaking through the instructor and that prayer in the church enables him to avoid the day's evil; any godly man ought to count it a great loss if he does not attend the place of instruction, especially if he can read.

If a (specially gifted) teacher should come, let none of you delay to attend the place where the instruction is given, for grace will be given to the speaker to utter things profitable to all, and thou wilt hear new things, and thou wilt be profited by what the Holy Spirit will give thee through the instructor; so thy faith will be strengthened by what thou hearest, and in that place thou wilt learn thy duties at home; therefore let everyone be zealous to go to the church, the place where the Holy Spirit abounds.

But if on any day there is no instruction, let everyone at home take the Bible and read sufficiently in passages that he finds profitable.

If at the third hour thou art at home, pray then and give thanks to God; but if thou chance to be abroad at that hour, make thy prayer to God in thy heart. For at that hour Christ was nailed to the tree; therefore in the old (covenant) the law commanded the showbread to be offered continually for a type of the body and blood of Christ, and commanded the sacrifice of the dumb lamb, which was a type of the perfect Lamb; for Christ is the Shepherd, and he is also the Bread that came down from heaven.

At the sixth hour likewise pray also, for, after Christ was nailed to the wood of the cross, the day was divided and there was a great darkness; wherefore let (the faithful) pray at that hour with an effectual prayer, likening themselves to the voice of him who prayed (and) caused all creation to become dark for the unbelieving Jews.

And at the ninth hour let a great prayer and a great thanksgiving be made, such as made the souls of the righteous ones, blessing the Lord, the God who does not lie, who was mindful of his saints and sent forth his Word to enlighten them. At that hour, therefore, Christ poured forth from his pierced side water and blood, and brought the rest of the time of that day with light to evening; so, when he fell asleep, by making the beginning of another day he completed the pattern of his resurrection.

Pray again before thy body rests on thy bed.

At midnight arise, wash thy hands with water and pray. And if thy wife is with thee, pray ye both together; but if she is not yet a believer, go into another room and pray, and again return to thy bed; be not slothful in prayer.

He who has used the marriage bed is not defiled; for they who are bathed have no need to wash again, for they are clean. By signing thyself with thy moist breath, and so spreading spittle on thy body with thy hand, thou art sanctified to thy feet; for the gift of the Spirit and the sprinkling with water, when it is brought with a believing heart as it were from a fountain, sanctifies him who believes.

It is needful to pray at this hour; for those very elders who gave us the tradition taught us that at this hour all creation rests for a certain moment, that all creatures may praise the Lord: stars and trees and waters stand still with one accord, and all the angelic host does service to God by praising Him, together with the souls of the righteous. For this cause believers should be zealous to pray at this hour; for the Lord, testifying to this, says: "Behold at midnight is a cry, Behold the Bridegroom cometh! Rise up to meet him!"; and he adds insistently: "Watch ye therefore, for ye know not at what hour he cometh".

And at cockcrow rise up and pray likewise, for at that hour of cockcrow the children of Israel denied Christ, whom we have known by faith; by which faith, in the hope of eternal life at the resurrection of the dead, we look for his Day.

And so, all ye faithful, if ye thus act, and are mindful of these things, and teach them to one another, and cause the catechumens to be zealous, ye can neither be tempted nor can ye perish, since ye have Christ always in your minds.

But imitate him always, by signing thy forehead sincerely; for this is the sign of his Passion, manifest and approved against the devil if so thou makest it from faith; not that thou mayest appear to men, but knowingly offering it as a shield. For the adversary, seeing its power coming from the heart, that a man displays the publicly formed image of baptism, is put to flight; not because thou spittest, but because the Spirit in thee breathes him away. When Moses formed it by putting the blood of the Paschal lamb that was slain on the lintel and anointing the side-posts, he signified the faith which now we have in the perfect Lamb.

And so, if these things are accepted with thanksgiving and right faith, they give edification in the church and eternal life to believers. I counsel that these things be kept by all who know aright; for over all who hear the apostolic tradition and keep it, no heretics or any other man will prevail to lead them astray. For the many heresies have increased because their leaders would not learn the purpose of the apostles but acted according to their own wills, following their lusts and not what was right.

Now, beloved, if we have omitted anything, God will reveal it to those who are worthy, guiding the holy church to its mooring in (God's) quiet haven.

Later Additions

On Saturday and Sunday the bishop shall whenever possible give the people the bread with his own hand, while the deacons break it. The presbyters too shall break the bread to be delivered; and whenever a deacon approaches a presbyter he shall hold out his robe, and the presbyter shall take the bread and deliver it to the people with his hand.

On other days they shall give the bread as the bishop determines.

In time of need the deacon shall be diligent in giving the blessed bread to the sick. If there is no presbyter to give out what is to be distributed, the deacon shall pronounce the thanksgiving and shall supervise those who carry it away, to make sure that they attend to their duty and (properly) distribute the blessed food; the distributors must give it to the widows and the sick. Whoever is entrusted with the duty by the church must distribute it on the same day; if he does not, he must (at least) do so on the next day with the addition of what is then given him. For (it is not his own property); it is given him only (in trust) as bread for the poor.

When evening has come and the bishop is present, the deacon shall bring in a lamp. Then the bishop, standing in the midst of the believers, before giving thanks shall first give the salutation:

The Lord be with you all.

And the people shall say:
(And) with thy spirit.

And the bishop shall say:
Let us give thanks to the Lord.

And the people shall say:

It is meet and right:
Majesty, exaltation and glory are due to Him.

But they shall not say "Lift up your hearts", for that belongs to the oblation. And he prays thus, saying:

We give thee thanks, O God, because thou hast enlightened us by revealing the incorruptible light. So we, having finished the length of a day, and being come to the beginning of the night, satisfied with the light of the day that thou hast created for our satisfaction; and now, since by thy grace we lack not a light for the evening, we sanctify thee and we glorify thee. Through thine only Son our Lord Jesus Christ, through whom be to thee with him glory and might and honour with the Holy Spirit, now, etc.

And they shall all say: Amen.

Then, rising up after supper, the children and virgins having prayed, they shall sing psalms. Then the deacon, holding the mixed cup of the offering, shall say a Hallelujah Psalm. Then, the presbyter having commanded, "And also such-and-such Psalms", after the bishop has offered the cup with the proper thanksgiving, all shall say "Hallelujah" as the Psalms are sung. [31]And they shall say:

We praise Him who is God most high;
Glorified and praised is He,
Who founded the world with a single word.

Then, when the Psalm is completed, he shall give thanks over the bread, and shall give the fragments to all the believers.

The faithful, early in the morning, as soon as they have awaked and arisen, before they undertake their tasks shall pray to God and so may then go to their duties. [2]But if any instruction in the word is held, let each give first place to that, that he may attend and hear the word of God, to his soul's comfort; so let each one hasten to the church, where the Spirit abounds.

But let each of the faithful be zealous, before he eats anything else, to receive the eucharist; for if anyone receives it with faith, after such a reception he cannot be harmed even if a deadly poison should be given him. But let each one take care that no unbeliever taste the eucharist, nor a mouse nor any other animal, and that nothing of it fall or be lost; for the body of Christ is to be eaten by believers and must not be despised. The cup, when thou hast given thanks in the name of the Lord, thou hast accepted as the image of the blood of Christ. Therefore let none of it be spilled, so that no alien spirit may lick it up, as if thou didst despise it; thou shalt be guilty of the blood, as if thou didst scorn the price with which thou hast been bought.